Black Decker Air Fry
Toaster Oven cookbook

800 Delicious and Affordable Air Fryer Recipes tailored for Your Black Decker Air Fryer Toaster Oven

Rose S. Alexander

Table of Contents

Chapter 3 Fish and Seafood

Chapter 4 Wraps and Sandwiches

Chapter 5 Vegan and Vegetarian

Chapter 6 Appetizers and Snacks

Chapter 7 Desserts

Chapter 8 Fast and Easy Everyday Favorites

Chapter 9 Holiday Specials

Appendix 1 Measurement Conversion Chart

Appendix 2 Air Fryer Cooking Chart

Appendix 3 Index

Chapter 1 Breakfast

Bell Pepper and Carrot Frittata

Prep time: 10 minutes | Cook time: 12 minutes | Serves 4

- ½ cup chopped red bell pepper
- ⅓ cup grated carrot
- ⅓ cup minced onion
- 1 teaspoon olive oil
- 1 egg
- 6 egg whites
- ⅓ cup 2% milk
- 1 tablespoon shredded Parmesan cheese

1. Mix together the red bell pepper, carrot, onion, and olive oil in a baking pan and stir to combine.

2. Select Bake. Set temperature to 350°F (180°C) and set time to 12 minutes. Press Start to begin preheating.

3. Once preheated, place the pan into the oven.

4. After 3 minutes, remove the pan from the oven. Stir the vegetables. Return the pan to the oven and continue cooking.

5. Meantime, whisk together the egg, egg whites, and milk in a medium bowl until creamy.

6. After 3 minutes, remove the pan from the oven. Pour the egg mixture over the top and scatter with the Parmesan cheese. Return the pan to the oven and continue cooking for additional 6 minutes.

7. When cooking is complete, the eggs will be set and the top will be golden around the edges.

8. Allow the frittata to cool for 5 minutes before slicing and serving.

Broccoli and Red Pepper Quiche

Prep time: 5 minutes | Cook time: 10 minutes | Serves 4

- 1 cup broccoli florets
- ¾ cup chopped roasted red peppers
- 1¼ cups grated Fontina cheese
- 6 eggs
- ¾ cup heavy cream
- ½ teaspoon salt
- Freshly ground black pepper, to taste
- Cooking spray

1. Spritz a baking pan with cooking spray

2. Add the broccoli florets and roasted red peppers to the pan and scatter the grated Fontina cheese on top.

3. In a bowl, beat together the eggs and heavy cream. Sprinkle with salt and pepper. Pour the egg mixture over the top of the cheese. Wrap the pan in foil.

4. Select Air Fry. Set temperature to 325°F (163°C) and set time to 10 minutes. Press Start to begin preheating.

5. Once preheated, place the pan into the oven.

6. After 8 minutes, remove the pan from the oven. Remove the foil. Return the pan to the oven and continue to cook another 2 minutes.

7. When cooked, the quiche should be golden brown.

8. Rest for 5 minutes before cutting into wedges and serve warm.

Vanilla Banana Bread Pudding

Prep time: 10 minutes | Cook time: 16 minutes | Serves 4

- 2 medium ripe bananas, mashed
- ½ cup low-fat milk
- 2 tablespoons maple syrup
- 2 tablespoons peanut butter
- 1 teaspoon vanilla extract
- 1 teaspoon ground cinnamon
- 2 slices whole-grain bread, cut into bite-sized cubes
- ¼ cup quick oats
- Cooking spray

1. Spritz a baking dish lightly with cooking spray.
2. Mix the bananas, milk, maple syrup, peanut butter, vanilla, and cinnamon in a large mixing bowl and stir until well incorporated.
3. Add the bread cubes to the banana mixture and stir until thoroughly coated. Fold in the oats and stir to combine.
4. Transfer the mixture to the baking dish. Wrap the baking dish in aluminum foil.
5. Select Air Fry. Set temperature to 350°F (180°C) and set time to 16 minutes. Press Start to begin preheating.
6. Once the oven has preheated, place the pan into the oven.
7. After 10 minutes, remove the baking dish from the oven. Remove the foil. Return the baking dish to the oven and continue to cook another 6 minutes.
8. When done, the pudding should be set.
9. Let the pudding cool for 5 minutes before serving.

Shrimp and Spinach Frittata

Prep time: 15 minutes | Cook time: 16 minutes | Serves 4

- 4 eggs
- Pinch salt
- ½ cup cooked rice
- ½ cup chopped cooked shrimp
- ½ cup baby spinach
- ½ cup grated Monterey Jack cheese
- Nonstick cooking spray

1. Spritz a baking pan with nonstick cooking spray.
2. Whisk the eggs and salt in a small bowl until frothy.
3. Place the cooked rice, shrimp, and baby spinach in the baking pan. Pour in the whisked eggs and scatter the cheese on top.
4. Select Bake. Set temperature to 320°F (160°C) and set time to 16 minutes. Press Start to begin preheating.
5. Once the oven has preheated, place the pan into the oven.
6. When cooking is complete, the frittata should be golden and puffy.
7. Let the frittata cool for 5 minutes before slicing to serve.

Cheddar Bacon Casserole

Prep time: 10 minutes | Cook time: 16 minutes | Serves 4

- 6 slices bacon
- 6 eggs
- Salt and pepper, to taste
- Cooking spray
- ½ cup chopped green bell
- pepper
- ½ cup chopped onion
- ¾ cup shredded Cheddar cheese

1. Place the bacon in a skillet over medium-high heat and cook each side for about 4 minutes until evenly crisp. Remove from the heat to a paper towel-lined plate to drain. Crumble it into small pieces and set aside.
2. Whisk the eggs with the salt and pepper in a medium bowl.
3. Spritz a baking pan with cooking spray.
4. Place the whisked eggs, crumbled bacon, green bell pepper, and onion in the prepared pan.
5. Select Bake. Set temperature to 400°F (205°C) and set time to 8 minutes. Press Start to begin preheating.
6. Once preheated, place the pan into the oven.
7. After 6 minutes, remove the pan from the oven. Scatter the Cheddar cheese all over. Return the pan to the oven and continue to cook another 2 minutes.
8. When cooking is complete, let sit for 5 minutes and serve on plates.

Cheddar Hash Brown Casserole

Prep time: 15 minutes | Cook time: 30 minutes | Serves 4

- 3½ cups frozen hash browns, thawed
- 1 teaspoon salt
- 1 teaspoon freshly ground black pepper
- 3 tablespoons butter, melted
- 1 (10.5-ounce / 298-g) can
- cream of chicken soup
- ½ cup sour cream
- 1 cup minced onion
- ½ cup shredded sharp Cheddar cheese
- Cooking spray

1. Put the hash browns in a large bowl and season with salt and black pepper. Add the melted butter, cream of chicken soup, and sour cream and stir until well incorporated. Mix in the minced onion and cheese and stir well.
2. Spray a baking pan with cooking spray.
3. Spread the hash brown mixture evenly into the baking pan.
4. Select Bake. Set temperature to 325°F (163°C) and set time to 30 minutes. Press Start to begin preheating.
5. Once the oven has preheated, place the pan into the oven.
6. When cooked, the hash brown mixture will be browned.
7. Cool for 5 minutes before serving.

Bell Pepper and Ham Omelet

Prep time: 5 minutes | Cook time: 20 minutes | Serves 2

- ¼ cup chopped bell pepper, green or red
- ¼ cup chopped onion
- ¼ cup diced ham
- 1 teaspoon butter
- 4 large eggs
- 2 tablespoons milk
- ⅛ teaspoon salt
- ¾ cup shredded sharp Cheddar cheese

1. Put the bell pepper, onion, ham, and butter in a baking pan and mix well.

2. Select Air Fry. Set temperature to 390°F (199°C) and set time to 5 minutes. Press Start to begin preheating.

3. Once the oven has preheated, place the pan into the oven.

4. After 1 minute, remove the pan from the oven. Stir the mixture. Return the pan to the oven and continue to cook for another 4 minutes.

5. When done, the veggies should be softened.

6. Whisk together the eggs, milk, and salt in a bowl. Pour the egg mixture over the veggie mixture.

7. Select Bake. Set temperature to 360°F (182°C) and set time to 15 minutes. place the pan into the oven.

8. After 14 minutes, remove the pan from the oven. Scatter the omelet with the shredded cheese. Return the pan to the oven and continue to cook for another 1 minute.

9. When cooking is complete, the top will be lightly golden browned, the eggs will be set and the cheese will be melled.

10. Let the omelet cool for 5 minutes before serving.

Mushroom and Spinach Frittata

Prep time: 10 minutes | Cook time: 22 minutes | Serves 2

- 4 large eggs
- 4 ounces (113 g) baby bella mushrooms, chopped
- 1 cup baby spinach, chopped
- ½ cup shredded Cheddar cheese
- ⅓ cup chopped leek, white part only
- ¼ cup halved grape
- tomatoes
- 1 tablespoon 2% milk
- ¼ teaspoon dried oregano
- ¼ teaspoon garlic powder
- ½ teaspoon kosher salt
- Freshly ground black pepper, to taste
- Cooking spray

1. Lightly spritz a baking dish with cooking spray.

2. Whisk the eggs in a large bowl until frothy. Add the mushrooms, baby spinach, cheese, leek, tomatoes, milk, oregano, garlic powder, salt, and pepper and stir until well blended. Pour the mixture into the prepared baking dish.

3. Select Bake. Set temperature to 300°F (150°C) and set time

to 22 minutes. Press Start to begin preheating.

4. Once the oven has preheated, place the dish into the oven.

5. When cooked, the center will be puffed up and the top will be golden brown.

6. Let the frittata cool for 5 minutes before slicing to serve.

Vanilla Pancake with Walnuts

Prep time: 10 minutes | Cook time: 20 minutes | Serves 4

- 3 tablespoons melted butter, divided
- 1 cup flour
- 2 tablespoons sugar
- 1½ teaspoons baking powder
- ¼ teaspoon salt
- 1 egg, beaten
- ¾ cup milk
- 1 teaspoon pure vanilla extract
- ½ cup roughly chopped walnuts
- Maple syrup or fresh sliced fruit, for serving

1. Grease a baking pan with 1 tablespoon of melted butter.

2. Mix together the flour, sugar, baking powder, and salt in a medium bowl. Add the beaten egg, milk, the remaining 2 tablespoons of melted butter, and vanilla and stir until the batter is sticky but slightly lumpy.

3. Slowly pour the batter into the greased baking pan and scatter with the walnuts.

4. Select Bake. Set temperature to 330°F (166°C) and set time to 20 minutes. Press Start to begin preheating.

5. Once preheated, place the pan into the oven.

6. When cooked, the pancake should be golden brown and cooked through.

7. Let the pancake rest for 5 minutes and serve topped with the maple syrup or fresh fruit, if desired.

Vanilla Pancake with Mixed Berries

Prep time: 10 minutes | Cook time: 14 minutes | Serves 4

- 1 tablespoon unsalted butter, at room temperature
- 1 egg
- 2 egg whites
- ½ cup 2% milk
- ½ cup whole-wheat pastry
- flour
- 1 teaspoon pure vanilla extract
- 1 cup sliced fresh strawberries
- ½ cup fresh raspberries
- ½ cup fresh blueberries

1. Grease a baking pan with the butter.

2. Using a hand mixer, beat together the egg, egg whites, milk, pastry flour, and vanilla in a medium mixing bowl until well incorporated.

3. Pour the batter into the pan.

4. Select Bake. Set temperature to 330°F (166°C) and set time

to 14 minutes. Press Start to begin preheating.

5. Once the oven has preheated, place the pan into the oven.

6. When cooked, the pancake should puff up in the center and the edges should be golden brown

7. Allow the pancake to cool for 5 minutes and serve topped with the berries.

Brown Rice Porridge with Dates

Prep time: 5 minutes | Cook time: 23 minutes | Serves 1 or 2

- ½ cup cooked brown rice
- 1 cup canned coconut milk
- ¼ cup unsweetened shredded coconut
- ¼ cup packed dark brown sugar
- 4 large Medjool dates,

- pitted and roughly chopped
- ½ teaspoon kosher salt
- ¼ teaspoon ground cardamom
- Heavy cream, for serving (optional)

1. Place all the ingredients except the heavy cream in a baking pan and stir until blended.

2. Select Bake. Set temperature to 375°F (190°C) and set time to 23 minutes. Press Start to begin preheating.

3. Once the oven has preheated, place the pan into the oven. Stir the porridge halfway through the cooking time.

4. When cooked, the porridge will be thick and creamy.

5. Remove from the oven and ladle the porridge into bowls.

6. Serve hot with a drizzle of the cream, if desired.

Vanilla Blueberry Cobbler

Prep time: 5 minutes | Cook time: 15 minutes | Serves 4

- ¾ teaspoon baking powder
- ⅓ cup whole-wheat pastry flour
- Dash sea salt
- ⅓ cup unsweetened nondairy milk
- 2 tablespoons maple syrup

- ½ teaspoon vanilla
- Cooking spray
- ½ cup blueberries
- ¼ cup granola
- Nondairy yogurt, for topping (optional)

1. Spritz a baking pan with cooking spray.

2. Mix together the baking powder, flour, and salt in a medium bowl. Add the milk, maple syrup, and vanilla and whisk to combine.

3. Scrape the mixture into the prepared pan. Scatter the blueberries and granola on top.

4. Select Bake. Set temperature to 347°F (175°C) and set time to 15 minutes. Press Start to begin preheating.

5. Once preheated, place the pan into the oven.

6. When done, the top should begin to brown and a knife inserted in the center should come out clean.

7. Let the cobbler cool for 5 minutes and serve with a drizzle of nondairy yogurt.

Asparagus Strata with Havarti Cheese

Prep time: 10 minutes | Cook time: 17 minutes | Serves 4

- 6 asparagus spears, cut into 2-inch pieces
- 1 tablespoon water
- 2 slices whole-wheat bread, cut into ½-inch cubes
- 4 eggs
- 3 tablespoons whole milk

- 2 tablespoons chopped flat-leaf parsley
- ½ cup grated Havarti or Swiss cheese
- Pinch salt
- Freshly ground black pepper, to taste
- Cooking spray

1. Add the asparagus spears and 1 tablespoon of water in a baking pan.

2. Select Bake. Set temperature to 330°F (166°C) and set time to 4 minutes. Press Start to begin preheating.

3. Once preheated, place the pan into the oven.

4. When cooking is complete, the asparagus spears will be crisp-tender.

5. Remove the asparagus from the pan and drain on paper towels.

6. Spritz the pan with cooking spray. Place the bread and asparagus in the pan.

7. Whisk together the eggs and milk in a medium mixing bowl until creamy. Fold in the parsley, cheese, salt, and pepper and stir to combine. Pour this mixture into the baking pan.

8. Select Bake and set time to 13 minutes. Place the pan back to the oven. When done, the eggs will be set and the top will be lightly browned.

9. Let cool for 5 minutes before slicing and serving.

Garlic Potatoes with Peppers and Onions

Prep time: 10 minutes | Cook time: 35 minutes | Serves 4

- 1 pound (454 g) red potatoes, cut into ½-inch dices
- 1 large red bell pepper, cut into ½-inch dices
- 1 large green bell pepper, cut into ½-inch dices
- 1 medium onion, cut into ½-inch dices

- 1½ tablespoons extra-virgin olive oil
- 1¼ teaspoons kosher salt
- ¾ teaspoon sweet paprika
- ¾ teaspoon garlic powder
- Freshly ground black pepper, to taste

1. Mix together the potatoes, bell peppers, onion, oil, salt, paprika, garlic powder, and black pepper in a large mixing and toss to coat.

2. Transfer the potato mixture to the perforated pan.

3. Select Air Fry. Set temperature to 350°F (180°C) and set time to 35 minutes. Press Start to begin preheating.

4. Once preheated, place the pan into the oven. Stir the potato mixture three times during cooking.

5. When done, the potatoes should be nicely browned.

6. Remove from the oven to a plate and serve warm.

Brown Rice Quiches with Pimiento

Prep time: 10 minutes | Cook time: 14 minutes | Serves 6

- 4 ounces (113 g) diced green chilies
- 3 cups cooked brown rice
- 1 cup shredded reduced-fat Cheddar cheese, divided
- ½ cup egg whites
- ⅓ cup fat-free milk
- ¼ cup diced pimiento
- ½ teaspoon cumin
- 1 small eggplant, cubed
- 1 bunch fresh cilantro, finely chopped
- Cooking spray

1. Spritz a 12-cup muffin pan with cooking spray.

2. In a large bowl, stir together all the ingredients, except for ½ cup of the cheese.

3. Scoop the mixture evenly into the muffin cups and sprinkle the remaining ½ cup of the cheese on top.

4. Select Bake. Set temperature to 400°F (205°C) and set time to 14 minutes. Press Start to begin preheating.

5. Once the unit has preheated, place the pan into the oven.

6. When cooking is complete, remove the pan and check the quiches. They should be set.

7. Carefully transfer the quiches to a platter and serve immediately.

Avocado and Egg Burrito

Prep time: 10 minutes | Cook time: 4 minutes | Serves 4

- 4 low-sodium whole-wheat flour tortillas

Filling:

- 1 hard-boiled egg, chopped
- 2 hard-boiled egg whites, chopped
- 1 ripe avocado, peeled, pitted, and chopped
- 1 red bell pepper, chopped
- 1 (1.2-ounce / 34-g) slice low-sodium, low-fat American cheese, torn into pieces
- 3 tablespoons low-sodium salsa, plus additional for serving (optional)

Special Equipment:

- 4 toothpicks (optional) soaked in water for at least 30 minutes

1. Make the filling: Combine the egg, egg whites, avocado, red bell pepper, cheese, and salsa in a medium bowl and stir until blended.

2. Assemble the burritos: Arrange the tortillas on a clean work surface and place ¼ of the prepared filling in the middle of each tortilla, leaving about 1½-inch on each end unfilled. Fold in the opposite sides of each tortilla and roll up. Secure with toothpicks through the center, if needed.

3. Transfer the burritos to the perforated pan.

4. Select Air Fry. Set temperature to 390°F (199°C) and set time to 4 minutes. Press Start to begin preheating.

5. Once the oven has preheated, place the pan into the oven.

6. When cooking is complete, the burritos should be crisp and golden brown.

7. Allow to cool for 5 minutes and serve with salsa, if desired.

Banana Chocolate Bread with Walnuts

Prep time: 10 minutes | Cook time: 30 minutes | Serves 4

- ¼ cup cocoa powder
- 6 tablespoons plus 2 teaspoons all-purpose flour, divided
- ½ teaspoon kosher salt
- ¼ teaspoon baking soda
- 1½ ripe bananas
- 1 large egg, whisked
- ¼ cup vegetable oil
- ½ cup sugar
- 3 tablespoons buttermilk or plain yogurt (not Greek)
- ½ teaspoon vanilla extract
- 6 tablespoons chopped white chocolate
- 6 tablespoons chopped walnuts

1. Mix together the cocoa powder, 6 tablespoons of the flour, salt, and baking soda in a medium bowl.

2. Mash the bananas with a fork in another medium bowl until smooth. Fold in the egg, oil, sugar, buttermilk, and vanilla, and whisk until thoroughly combined. Add the wet mixture to the dry mixture and stir until well incorporated.

3. Combine the white chocolate, walnuts, and the remaining 2 tablespoons of flour in a third bowl and toss to coat. Add this mixture to the batter and stir until well incorporated. Pour the batter into a baking pan and smooth the top with a spatula.

4. Select Bake. Set temperature to 310°F (154°C) and set time to 30 minutes. Press Start to begin preheating.

5. Once the oven has preheated, place the pan into the oven.

6. When done, a toothpick inserted into the center of the bread should come out clean.

7. Remove from the oven and allow to cool on a wire rack for 10 minutes before serving.

Baked Eggs with Kale Pesto

Prep time: 5 minutes | Cook time: 11 minutes | Serves 2

- 1 cup roughly chopped kale leaves, stems and center ribs removed
- ¼ cup grated pecorino cheese
- ¼ cup olive oil

- 1 garlic clove, peeled
- 3 tablespoons whole almonds
- Kosher salt and freshly ground black pepper, to taste
- 4 large eggs
- 2 tablespoons heavy cream
- 3 tablespoons chopped pitted mixed olives

1. Place the kale, pecorino, olive oil, garlic, almonds, salt, and pepper in a small blender and blitz until well incorporated.

2. One at a time, crack the eggs in a baking pan. Drizzle the kale pesto on top of the egg whites. Top the yolks with the cream and swirl together the yolks and the pesto.

3. Select Bake. Set temperature to 300°F (150°C) and set time to 11 minutes. Press Start to begin preheating.

4. Once preheated, place the pan into the oven.

5. When cooked, the top should begin to brown and the eggs should be set.

6. Allow the eggs to cool for 5 minutes. Scatter the olives on top and serve warm.

Chicken Breakfast Sausages

Prep time: 15 minutes | Cook time: 10 minutes | Makes 8 patties

- 1 Granny Smith apple, peeled and finely chopped
- 2 tablespoons apple juice
- 2 garlic cloves, minced
- 1 egg white
- ⅓ cup minced onion
- 3 tablespoons ground almonds
- ⅛ teaspoon freshly ground black pepper
- 1 pound (454 g) ground chicken breast

1. Combine all the ingredients except the chicken in a medium mixing bowl and stir well.

2. Add the chicken breast to the apple mixture and mix with your hands until well incorporated.

3. Divide the mixture into 8 equal portions and shape into patties. Arrange the patties in the perforated pan.

4. Select Air Fry. Set temperature to 330°F (166°C) and set time to 10 minutes. Press Start to begin preheating.

5. Once the oven has preheated, place the pan into the oven.

6. When done, a meat thermometer inserted in the center of the chicken should reach at least 165°F (74°C).

7. Remove from the oven to a plate. Let the chicken cool for 5 minutes and serve warm.

Blueberries Quesadillas

Prep time: 5 minutes | Cook time: 4 minutes | Serves 2

- ¼ cup nonfat Ricotta cheese
- ¼ cup plain nonfat Greek yogurt
- 2 tablespoons finely ground flaxseeds
- 1 tablespoon granulated stevia

- ½ teaspoon cinnamon
- ¼ teaspoon vanilla extract
- 2 (8-inch) low-carb whole-
- wheat tortillas
- ½ cup fresh blueberries, divided

1. Line the sheet pan with the aluminum foil.

2. In a small bowl, whisk together the Ricotta cheese, yogurt, flaxseeds, stevia, cinnamon and vanilla.

3. Place the tortillas on the sheet pan. Spread half of the yogurt mixture on each tortilla, almost to the edges. Top each tortilla with ¼ cup of blueberries. Fold the tortillas in half.

4. Select Bake. Set temperature to 400°F (205°C) and set time to 4 minutes. Press Start to begin preheating.

5. Once the unit has preheated, place the pan into the oven.

6. When cooking is complete, remove the pan from the oven. Serve immediately.

Banana Bread

Prep time: 10 minutes | Cook time: 22 minutes | Makes 3 loaves

- 3 ripe bananas, mashed
- 1 cup sugar
- 1 large egg
- 4 tablespoons (½ stick)
- unsalted butter, melted
- 1½ cups all-purpose flour
- 1 teaspoon baking soda
- 1 teaspoon salt

1. Coat the insides of 3 mini loaf pans with cooking spray.

2. In a large mixing bowl, mix the bananas and sugar.

3. In a separate large mixing bowl, combine the egg, butter, flour, baking soda, and salt and mix well.

4. Add the banana mixture to the egg and flour mixture. Mix well.

5. Divide the batter evenly among the prepared pans.

6. Place the loaf pans on the bake position. Select Bake, set the temperature to 310°F (154°C), and set the time to 22 minutes.

7. Bake for 22 minutes. Insert a toothpick into the center of each loaf; if it comes out clean, they are done.

8. When the loaves are cooked through, remove the pans from the grill. Turn out the loaves onto a wire rack to cool.

9. Serve warm.

Sausage and Cheese Quiche

Prep time: 5 minutes | Cook time: 25 minutes | Serves 4

- 12 large eggs
- 1 cup heavy cream
- Salt and black pepper, to taste
- 12 ounces (340 g) sugar-
- free breakfast sausage
- 2 cups shredded Cheddar cheese
- Cooking spray

1. Coat a casserole dish with cooking spray.

2. Place the casserole dish on the bake position. Select Bake, set the temperature to 375°F (191°C), and set the time to 25 minutes.

3. Beat together the eggs, heavy cream, salt and pepper in a large bowl until creamy. Stir in the breakfast sausage and Cheddar cheese.

4. Pour the sausage mixture into the prepared casserole dish. Place the dish directly in the pan. Bake for 25 minutes, or until the top of the quiche is golden brown and the eggs are set.

5. Remove from the grill and let sit for 5 to 10 minutes before serving.

Crustless Broccoli Quiche

Prep time: 5 minutes | Cook time: 10 minutes | Serves 4

- 1 cup broccoli florets
- ¾ cup chopped roasted red peppers
- 1¼ cups grated Fontina cheese
- 6 eggs
- ¾ cup heavy cream
- ½ teaspoon salt
- Freshly ground black pepper, to taste
- Cooking spray

1. Spritz the baking pan with cooking spray.

2. Place the baking pan on the air fry position. Select Air Fry, set the temperature to 325°F (163°C), and set the time to 10 minutes.

3. Add the broccoli florets and roasted red peppers to the pan and scatter the grated Fontina cheese on top.

4. In a bowl, beat together the eggs and heavy cream. Sprinkle with salt and pepper. Pour the egg mixture over the top of the cheese. Wrap the pan in foil.

5. Air fry for 8 minutes. Remove the foil and continue to cook another 2 minutes until the quiche is golden brown.

6. Rest for 5 minutes before cutting into wedges and serve warm.

Cheesy Breakfast Casserole

Prep time: 10 minutes | Cook time: 14 minutes | Serves 4

- 6 slices bacon
- 6 eggs
- Salt and pepper, to taste
- Cooking spray
- ½ cup chopped green bell
- pepper
- ½ cup chopped onion
- ¾ cup shredded Cheddar cheese

1. Place the bacon in a skillet over medium-high heat and cook each side for about 4 minutes until evenly crisp. Remove from the heat to a paper towel-lined plate to drain. Crumble it into small pieces and set aside.

2. Whisk the eggs with the salt and pepper in a medium bowl.

3. Place the baking pan on the bake position. Select Bake, set the temperature to 400°F (204°C), and set the time to 8 minutes.

4. Spritz the baking pan with cooking spray.

5. Place the whisked eggs, crumbled bacon, green bell pepper, and onion in the prepared pan. Bake for 6 minutes.

6. Scatter the Cheddar cheese all over and bake for 2 minutes more.

7. Allow to sit for 5 minutes and serve on plates.

Cheesy Hash Brown Casserole

Prep time: 15 minutes | Cook time: 30 minutes | Serves 4

- 3½ cups frozen hash browns, thawed
- 1 teaspoon salt
- 1 teaspoon freshly ground black pepper
- 3 tablespoons butter, melted
- 1 (10.5-ounce / 298-g) can
- cream of chicken soup
- ½ cup sour cream
- 1 cup minced onion
- ½ cup shredded sharp Cheddar cheese
- Cooking spray

1. Put the hash browns in a large bowl and season with salt and black pepper. Add the melted butter, cream of chicken soup, and sour cream and stir until well incorporated. Mix in the minced onion and cheese and stir well.

2. Place the baking pan on the bake position. Select Bake, set the temperature to 325°F (163°C), and set the time to 30 minutes.

3. Spray the baking pan with cooking spray.

4. Spread the hash brown mixture evenly into the baking pan.

5. Bake for 30 minutes until browned.

6. Cool for 5 minutes before serving.

Breakfast Tater Tot Casserole

Prep time: 5 minutes | Cook time: 17 to 19 minutes | Serves 4

- 4 eggs
- 1 cup milk
- Salt and pepper, to taste
- 12 ounces (340 g) ground chicken sausage
- 1 pound (454 g) frozen tater tots, thawed
- ¾ cup grated Cheddar cheese
- Cooking spray

1. Whisk together the eggs and milk in a medium bowl. Season with salt and pepper to taste and stir until mixed. Set aside.

2. Place a skillet over medium-high heat and spritz with cooking spray. Place the ground sausage in the skillet and break it into smaller pieces with a spatula or spoon. Cook for 3 to 4 minutes until the sausage starts to brown, stirring occasionally. Remove from heat and set aside.

3. Place the baking pan on the bake position. Select Bake, set the temperature to 400°F (204°C), and set the time to 15 minutes.

4. Coat the baking pan with cooking spray.

5. Arrange the tater tots in the baking pan. Bake for 15 minutes. Stir in the egg mixture and cooked sausage. Bake for another 6 minutes.

6. Scatter the cheese on top of the tater tots. Continue to bake for 2 to 3 minutes more until the cheese is bubbly and melted.

7. Let the mixture cool for 5 minutes and serve warm.

Western Omelet

Prep time: 5 minutes | Cook time: 18 to 21 minutes | Serves 2

- ¼ cup chopped bell pepper, green or red
- ¼ cup chopped onion
- ¼ cup diced ham
- 1 teaspoon butter
- 4 large eggs
- 2 tablespoons milk
- ⅛ teaspoon salt
- ¾ cup shredded sharp Cheddar cheese

1. Place the baking pan on the air fry position. Select Air Fry, set the temperature to 390°F (199°C), and set the time to 6 minutes.

2. Put the bell pepper, onion, ham, and butter in the baking pan and mix well.

3. Air fry for 1 minute. Stir and continue to cook for an additional 4 to 5 minutes until the veggies are softened.

4. Meanwhile, whisk together the eggs, milk, and salt in a bowl.

5. Pour the egg mixture over the veggie mixture.

6. Reduce the grill temperature to 360°F (182°C) and bake for 13 to 15 minutes more, or until the top is lightly golden browned and the eggs are set.

7. Scatter the omelet with the shredded cheese. Bake for another 1 minute until the cheese has melted.

8. Let the omelet cool for 5 minutes before serving.

Spinach, Leek and Cheese Frittata

Prep time: 10 minutes | Cook time: 20 to 23 minutes | Serves 2

- 4 large eggs
- 4 ounces (113 g) baby bella mushrooms, chopped
- 1 cup (1 ounce / 28-g) baby spinach, chopped
- ½ cup (2 ounces / 57-g) shredded Cheddar cheese
- ⅓ cup (from 1 large) chopped leek, white part
- only
- ¼ cup halved grape tomatoes
- 1 tablespoon 2% milk
- ¼ teaspoon dried oregano
- ¼ teaspoon garlic powder
- ½ teaspoon kosher salt
- Freshly ground black

pepper, to taste
- Cooking spray

1. Place the baking pan on the bake position. Select Bake, set the temperature to 300°F (149°C), and set the time to 23 minutes.

2. Lightly spritz the baking pan with cooking spray.

3. Whisk the eggs in a large bowl until frothy. Add the mushrooms, baby spinach, cheese, leek, tomatoes, milk, oregano, garlic powder, salt, and pepper and stir until well blended. Pour the mixture into the prepared baking pan.

4. Bake for 20 to 23 minutes, or until the center is puffed up and the top is golden brown.

5. Let the frittata cool for 5 minutes before slicing to serve.

Veggie Frittata

Prep time: 10 minutes | Cook time: 8 to 12 minutes | Serves 4

- ½ cup chopped red bell pepper
- ⅓ cup grated carrot
- ⅓ cup minced onion
- 1 teaspoon olive oil
- 1 egg
- 6 egg whites
- ⅓ cup 2% milk
- 1 tablespoon shredded Parmesan cheese

1. Place the baking pan on the bake position. Select Bake, set the temperature to 350°F (177°C), and set the time to 12 minutes.

2. Mix together the red bell pepper, carrot, onion, and olive oil in the baking pan and stir to combine.

3. Bake for 4 to 6 minutes, or until the veggies are soft. Stir once during cooking.

4. Meantime, whisk together the egg, egg whites, and milk in a medium bowl until creamy.

5. When the veggies are done, pour the egg mixture over the top. Scatter with the Parmesan cheese.

6. Bake for an additional 4 to 6 minutes, or until the eggs are set and the top is golden around the edges.

7. Allow the frittata to cool for 5 minutes before slicing and serving.

Tomato-Corn Frittata with Avocado Dressing

Prep time: 10 minutes | Cook time: 20 minutes | Serves 2 or 3

- ½ cup cherry tomatoes, halved
- Kosher salt and freshly ground black pepper, to taste
- 6 large eggs, lightly beaten
- ½ cup corn kernels, thawed if frozen
- ¼ cup milk
- 1 tablespoon finely chopped fresh dill
- ½ cup shredded Monterey Jack cheese

Avocado Dressing:
- 1 ripe avocado, pitted and peeled
- 2 tablespoons fresh lime juice

- ¼ cup olive oil
- 1 scallion, finely chopped
- 8 fresh basil leaves, finely chopped

1. Put the tomato halves in a colander and lightly season with salt. Set aside for 10 minutes to drain well. Pour the tomatoes into a large bowl and fold in the eggs, corn, milk, and dill. Sprinkle with salt and pepper and stir until mixed.

2. Place the baking pan on the bake position. Select Bake, set the temperature to 300°F (149°C), and set the time to 20 minutes.

3. Pour the egg mixture into the baking pan. Bake for 15 minutes.

4. Scatter the cheese on top. Increase the grill temperature to 315°F (157°C) and continue to cook for another 5 minutes, or until the frittata is puffy and set.

5. Meanwhile, make the avocado dressing: Mash the avocado with the lime juice in a medium bowl until smooth. Mix in the olive oil, scallion, and basil and stir until well incorporated.

6. Let the frittata cool for 5 minutes and serve alongside the avocado dressing.

Maple Walnut Pancake

Prep time: 10 minutes | Cook time: 20 minutes | Serves 4

- 3 tablespoons melted butter, divided
- 1 cup flour
- 2 tablespoons sugar
- 1½ teaspoons baking powder
- ¼ teaspoon salt
- 1 egg, beaten
- ¾ cup milk
- 1 teaspoon pure vanilla extract
- ½ cup roughly chopped walnuts
- Maple syrup or fresh sliced fruit, for serving

1. Place the baking pan on the bake position. Select Bake, set the temperature to 330°F (166°C), and set the time to 20 minutes.

2. Grease the baking pan with 1 tablespoon of melted butter.

3. Mix together the flour, sugar, baking powder, and salt in a medium bowl. Add the beaten egg, milk, the remaining 2 tablespoons of melted butter, and vanilla and stir until the batter is sticky but slightly lumpy.

4. Slowly pour the batter into the greased baking pan and scatter with the walnuts.

5. Bake for 20 minutes until golden brown and cooked through.

6. Let the pancake rest for 5 minutes and serve topped with the maple syrup or fresh fruit, if desired.

Mixed Berry Dutch Baby Pancake

Prep time: 10 minutes | Cook time: 12 to 16 minutes | Serves 4

- 1 tablespoon unsalted butter, at room temperature
- 1 egg
- 2 egg whites
- ½ cup 2% milk
- ½ cup whole-wheat pastry
- flour
- 1 teaspoon pure vanilla extract
- 1 cup sliced fresh strawberries
- ½ cup fresh raspberries
- ½ cup fresh blueberries

1. Place the baking pan on the bake position. Select Bake, set the temperature to 330°F (166°C), and set the time to 16 minutes.

2. Grease the baking pan with the butter.

3. Using a hand mixer, beat together the egg, egg whites, milk, pastry flour, and vanilla in a medium mixing bowl until well incorporated.

4. Pour the batter into the pan. Bake for 12 to 16 minutes, or until the pancake puffs up in the center and the edges are golden brown.

5. Allow the pancake to cool for 5 minutes and serve topped with the berries.

Bacon and Egg Bread Cups

Prep time: 10 minutes | Cook time: 8 to 12 minutes | Serves 4

- 4 (3-by-4-inch) crusty rolls
- 4 thin slices Gouda or Swiss cheese mini wedges
- 5 eggs
- 2 tablespoons heavy cream
- 3 strips precooked bacon, chopped
- ½ teaspoon dried thyme
- Pinch salt
- Freshly ground black pepper, to taste

1. Place the baking pan on the bake position. Select Bake, set the temperature to 330°F (166°C), and set the time to 12 minutes.

2. On a clean work surface, cut the tops off the rolls. Using your fingers, remove the insides of the rolls to make bread cups, leaving a ½-inch shell. Place a slice of cheese onto each roll bottom.

3. Whisk together the eggs and heavy cream in a medium bowl until well combined. Fold in the bacon, thyme, salt, and pepper and stir well.

4. Scrape the egg mixture into the prepared bread cups.

5. Place the bread cups directly in the pan. Bake for 8 to 12 minutes, or until the eggs are cooked to your preference.

6. Serve warm.

Banana and Oat Bread Pudding

Prep time: 10 minutes | Cook time: 16 to 20 minutes | Serves 4

- 2 medium ripe bananas, mashed
- ½ cup low-fat milk
- 2 tablespoons maple syrup

- 2 tablespoons peanut butter
- 1 teaspoon vanilla extract
- 1 teaspoon ground cinnamon
- 2 slices whole-grain bread, cut into bite-sized cubes
- ¼ cup quick oats
- Cooking spray

1. Spritz the baking pan lightly with cooking spray.

2. Place the baking pan on the air fry position. Select Air Fry, set the temperature to 350°F (177°C), and set the time to 20 minutes.

3. Mix the bananas, milk, maple syrup, peanut butter, vanilla, and cinnamon in a large mixing bowl and stir until well incorporated.

4. Add the bread cubes to the banana mixture and stir until thoroughly coated. Fold in the oats and stir to combine.

5. Transfer the mixture to the baking pan. Wrap the baking pan in aluminum foil.

6. Air fry for 10 to 12 minutes until heated through.

7. Remove the foil and cook for an additional 6 to 8 minutes, or until the pudding has set.

8. Let the pudding cool for 5 minutes before serving.

Coconut Brown Rice Porridge with Dates

Prep time: 5 minutes | Cook time: 23 minutes | Serves 1 or 2

- ½ cup cooked brown rice
- 1 cup canned coconut milk
- ¼ cup unsweetened shredded coconut
- ¼ cup packed dark brown sugar
- 4 large Medjool dates,
- pitted and roughly chopped
- ½ teaspoon kosher salt
- ¼ teaspoon ground cardamom
- Heavy cream, for serving (optional)

1. Place the baking pan on the bake position. Select Bake, set the temperature to 375°F (191°C), and set the time to 23 minutes.

2. Place all the ingredients except the heavy cream in the baking pan and stir until blended.

3. Bake for 23 minutes until the porridge is thick and creamy. Stir the porridge halfway through the cooking time.

4. Remove from the grill and ladle the porridge into bowls.

5. Serve hot with a drizzle of the cream, if desired.

Fried Potatoes with Peppers and Onions

Prep time: 10 minutes | Cook time: 35 minutes | Serves 4

- 1 pound (454 g) red panatoes, cut into ½-inch dices
- 1 large red bell pepper, cut into ½-inch dices
- 1 large green bell pepper, cut into ½-inch dices
- 1 medium onion, cut into ½-inch dices
- 1½ tablespoons extra-

virgin olive oil
- 1¼ teaspoons kosher salt
- ¾ teaspoon sweet paprika
- ¾ teaspoon garlic powder
- Freshly ground black pepper, to taste

1. Place the crisper tray on the air fry position. Select Air Fry, set the temperature to 350°F (177°C), and set the time to 35 minutes.

2. Mix together the panatoes, bell peppers, onion, oil, salt, paprika, garlic powder, and black pepper in a large mixing and toss to coat.

3. Transfer the panato mixture to the crisper tray. Air fry for 35 minutes, or until the panatoes are nicely browned. Shake the crisper tray three times during cooking.

4. Remove from the crisper tray to a plate and serve warm.

Olives, Kale, and Pecorino Baked Eggs

Prep time: 5 minutes | Cook time: 10 to 12 minutes | Serves 2

- 1 cup roughly chopped kale leaves, stems and center ribs removed
- ¼ cup grated pecorino cheese
- ¼ cup olive oil
- 1 garlic clove, peeled
- 3 tablespoons whole almonds
- Kosher salt and freshly ground black pepper, to taste
- 4 large eggs
- 2 tablespoons heavy cream
- 3 tablespoons chopped pitted mixed olives

1. Place the kale, pecorino, olive oil, garlic, almonds, salt, and pepper in a small blender and blitz until well incorporated.

2. Place the baking pan on the bake position. Select Bake, set the temperature to 300°F (149°C), and set the time to 12 minutes.

3. One at a time, crack the eggs in the baking pan. Drizzle the kale pesto on top of the egg whites. Top the yolks with the cream and swirl together the yolks and the pesto.

4. Bake for 10 to 12 minutes, or until the top begins to brown and the eggs are set.

5. Allow the eggs to cool for 5 minutes. Scatter the olives on top and serve warm.

Asparagus and Cheese Strata

Prep time: 10 minutes | Cook time: 14 to 19 minutes | Serves 4

- 6 asparagus spears, cut into 2-inch pieces
- 1 tablespoon water
- 2 slices whole-wheat bread, cut into ½-inch cubes
- 4 eggs
- 3 tablespoons whole milk
- 2 tablespoons chopped flat-leaf parsley
- ½ cup grated Havarti or Swiss cheese
- Pinch salt
- Freshly ground black pepper, to taste
- Cooking spray

1. Place the baking pan on the bake position. Select Bake, set the temperature to 330°F (166°C), and set the time to 19 minutes.

2. Add the asparagus spears and 1 tablespoon of water in the baking pan. Bake for 3 to 5 minutes until crisp-tender. Remove the asparagus from the pan and drain on paper towels. Spritz the pan with cooking spray.

3. Place the bread and asparagus in the pan.

4. Whisk together the eggs and milk in a medium mixing bowl until creamy. Fold in the parsley, cheese, salt, and pepper and stir to combine. Pour this mixture into the baking pan.

5. Bake for 11 to 14 minutes, or until the eggs are set and the top is lightly browned.

6. Let cool for 5 minutes before slicing and serving.

Egg and Avocado Burrito

Prep time: 10 minutes | Cook time: 3 to 5 minutes | Serves 4

- 4 low-sodium whole-wheat flour tortillas

Filling:

- 1 hard-boiled egg, chopped
- 2 hard-boiled egg whites, chopped
- 1 ripe avocado, peeled, pitted, and chopped
- 1 red bell pepper, chopped
- 1 (1.2-ounce / 34-g) slice low-sodium, low-fat American cheese, torn into pieces
- 3 tablespoons low-sodium salsa, plus additional for serving (optional)

Special Equipment:

1. 4 toothpicks (optional), soaked in water for at least 30 minutes

2. Place the crisper tray on the air fry position. Select Air Fry, set the temperature to 390°F (199°C), and set the time to 5 minutes.

3. Make the filling: Combine the egg, egg whites, avocado, red bell pepper, cheese, and salsa in a medium bowl and stir until blended.

4. Assemble the burritos: Arrange the tortillas on a clean work surface and place ¼ of the prepared filling in the middle of each tortilla, leaving about 1½-inch on each end unfilled. Fold in the opposite sides of each tortilla and roll up. Secure with toothpicks through the center, if needed.

5. Transfer the burritos to the crisper tray. Air fry for 3 to 5 minutes, or until the burritos are crisp and golden brown.

6. Allow to cool for 5 minutes and serve with salsa, if desired.

Chapter 2 Poultry

Lime Chicken Breasts with Cilantro

Prep time: 35 minutes | Cook time: 10 minutes | Serves 4

- 4 (4-ounce / 113-g) boneless, skinless chicken breasts
- ½ cup chopped fresh cilantro
- Juice of 1 lime
- Chicken seasoning or rub, to taste
- Salt and ground black pepper, to taste
- Cooking spray

1. Put the chicken breasts in the large bowl, then add the cilantro, lime juice, chicken seasoning, salt, and black pepper. Toss to coat well.

2. Wrap the bowl in plastic and refrigerate to marinate for at least 30 minutes.

3. Spritz the perforated pan with cooking spray.

4. Remove the marinated chicken breasts from the bowl and place in the perforated pan. Spritz with cooking spray.

5. Select Air Fry. Set temperature to 400°F (205°C) and set time to 10 minutes. Press Start to begin preheating.

6. Once preheated, place the pan into the oven. Flip the breasts halfway through.

7. When cooking is complete, the internal temperature of the chicken should reach at least 165°F (74°C).

8. Serve immediately.

Ground Chicken with Tomatoes

Prep time: 5 minutes | Cook time: 17 minutes | Serves 2

- 2 red bell peppers, chopped
- 1 pound (454 g) ground chicken
- 2 medium tomatoes, diced
- ½ cup chicken broth
- Salt and ground black pepper, to taste
- Cooking spray

1. Spritz a baking pan with cooking spray.

2. Set the bell pepper in the baking pan.

3. Select Broil. Set temperature to 365°F (185°C) and set time to 5 minutes. Press Start to begin preheating.

4. Once preheated, place the pan into the oven. Stir the bell pepper halfway through.

5. When broiling is complete, the bell pepper should be tender.

6. Add the ground chicken and diced tomatoes in the baking pan and stir to mix well.

7. Set time to 12 minutes. Stir the mixture and mix in the chicken broth, salt and ground black pepper halfway through.

8. When cooking is complete, the chicken should be well browned.

9. Serve immediately.

Chicken with Veggie Couscous Salad

Prep time: 25 minutes | Cook time: 20 minutes | Serves 4

- 3 tablespoons plus 2 teaspoons pomegranate molasses
- ½ teaspoon ground cinnamon
- 1 teaspoon minced fresh thyme
- Salt and ground black pepper, to taste
- 2 (12-ounce / 340-g) bone-in split chicken breasts, trimmed
- ¼ cup chicken broth
- ¼ cup water
- ½ cup couscous
- 1 tablespoon minced fresh parsley
- 2 ounces (57 g) cherry tomatoes, quartered
- 1 scallion, white part minced, green part sliced thin on bias
- 1 tablespoon extra-virgin olive oil
- 1 ounce (28 g) feta cheese, crumbled
- Cooking spray

1. Spritz the perforated pan with cooking spray.
2. Combine 3 tablespoons of pomegranate molasses, cinnamon, thyme, and ⅛ teaspoon of salt in a small bowl. Stir to mix well. Set aside.
3. Place the chicken breasts in the perforated pan, skin side down, and spritz with cooking spray. Sprinkle with salt and ground black pepper.
4. Select Air Fry. Set temperature to 350°F (180°C) and set time to 20 minutes. Press Start to begin preheating.
5. Once preheated, place the pan into the oven. Flip the chicken and brush with pomegranate molasses mixture halfway through.
6. Meanwhile, pour the broth and water in a pot and bring to a boil over medium-high heat. Add the couscous and sprinkle with salt. Cover and simmer for 7 minutes or until the liquid is almost absorbed.
7. Combine the remaining ingredients, except for the cheese, with cooked couscous in a large bowl. Toss to mix well. Scatter with the feta cheese.
8. When cooking is complete, remove the chicken from the oven and allow to cool for 10 minutes. Serve with vegetable and couscous salad.

Chicken Thighs with Mirin

Prep time: 10 minutes | Cook time: 15 minutes | Serves 4

- ½ cup mirin
- ¼ cup dry white wine
- ½ cup soy sauce
- 1 tablespoon light brown sugar
- 1½ pounds (680 g) boneless, skinless chicken thighs, cut into 1½-inch pieces, fat trimmed
- 4 medium scallions, trimmed, cut into 1½-inch pieces
- Cooking spray

Special Equipment:

- 4 (4-inch) bamboo skewers, soaked in water for at least 30 minutes

1. Combine the mirin, dry white wine, soy sauce, and brown sugar in a saucepan. Bring to a boil over medium heat. Keep stirring.
2. Boil for another 2 minutes or until it has a thick consistency. Turn off the heat.
3. Spritz the perforated pan with cooking spray.
4. Run the bamboo skewers through the chicken pieces and scallions alternatively.
5. Arrange the skewers in the perforated pan, then brush with mirin mixture on both sides. Spritz with cooking spray.
6. Select Air Fry. Set temperature to 400°F (205°C) and set time to 10 minutes. Press Start to begin preheating.
7. Once preheated, place the pan into the oven. Flip the skewers halfway through.
8. When cooking is complete, the chicken and scallions should be glossy.
9. Serve immediately.

Garlicky Whole Chicken Bake

Prep time: 10 minutes | Cook time: 1 hour | Serves 2 to 4

- ½ cup melted butter
- 3 tablespoons garlic, minced
- Salt, to taste
- 1 teaspoon ground black pepper
- 1 (1-pound / 454-g) whole chicken

1. Combine the butter with garlic, salt, and ground black pepper in a small bowl.
2. Brush the butter mixture over the whole chicken, then place the chicken in the perforated pan, skin side down.
3. Select Bake. Set temperature to 350°F (180°C) and set time to 60 minutes. Press Start to begin preheating.
4. Once preheated, place the pan into the oven. Flip the chicken halfway through.
5. When cooking is complete, an instant-read thermometer inserted in the thickest part of the chicken should register at least 165°F (74°C).
6. Remove the chicken from the oven and allow to cool for 15 minutes before serving.

Garlic Chicken Wings

Prep time: 10 minutes | Cook time: 15 minutes | Serves 4

- 1 tablespoon olive oil
- 8 whole chicken wings
- Chicken seasoning or rub, to taste
- 1 teaspoon garlic powder
- Freshly ground black pepper, to taste

1. Grease the perforated pan with olive oil.
2. On a clean work surface, rub the chicken wings with

chicken seasoning and rub, garlic powder, and ground black pepper.

3. Arrange the well-coated chicken wings in the perforated pan.

4. Select Air Fry. Set temperature to 400°F (205°C) and set time to 15 minutes. Press Start to begin preheating.

5. Once preheated, place the pan into the oven. Flip the chicken wings halfway through.

6. When cooking is complete, the internal temperature of the chicken wings should reach at least 165°F (74°C).

7. Remove the chicken wings from the oven. Serve immediately.

Chicken and Pepper Baguette with Mayo

Prep time: 10 minutes | Cook time: 20 minutes | Serves 2

- 1¼ pounds (567 g) assorted small chicken parts, breasts cut into halves
- ¼ teaspoon salt
- ¼ teaspoon ground black pepper
- 2 teaspoons olive oil
- ½ pound (227 g) mini sweet
- peppers
- ¼ cup light mayonnaise
- ¼ teaspoon smoked paprika
- ½ clove garlic, crushed
- Baguette, for serving
- Cooking spray

1. Spritz the perforated pan with cooking spray.

2. Toss the chicken with salt, ground black pepper, and olive oil in a large bowl.

3. Arrange the sweet peppers and chicken in the perforated pan.

4. Select Air Fry. Set temperature to 375°F (190°C) and set time to 20 minutes. Press Start to begin preheating.

5. Once preheated, place the pan into the oven. Flip the chicken and transfer the peppers on a plate halfway through.

6. When cooking is complete, the chicken should be well browned.

7. Meanwhile, combine the mayo, paprika, and garlic in a small bowl. Stir to mix well.

8. Assemble the baguette with chicken and sweet pepper, then spread with mayo mixture and serve.

Satay Chicken Skewers

Prep time: 5 minutes | Cook time: 10 minutes | Serves 4

- 4 (6-ounce / 170-g) boneless, skinless chicken breasts, sliced into strips
- 1 teaspoon sea salt
- 1 teaspoon paprika
- Cooking spray

Satay Sauce:
- ¼ cup creamy almond butter
- ½ teaspoon hot sauce
- 1½ tablespoons coconut vinegar

- 2 tablespoons chicken broth
- 1 teaspoon peeled and minced fresh ginger
- 1 clove garlic, minced
- 1 teaspoon sugar

For Serving:
- ¼ cup chopped cilantro

- leaves
- Red pepper flakes, to taste
- Thinly sliced red, orange, or / and yellow bell peppers

Special Equipment:
- 16 wooden or bamboo skewers, soaked in water for 15 minutes

1. Spritz the perforated pan with cooking spray.

2. Run the bamboo skewers through the chicken strips, then arrange the chicken skewers in the perforated pan and sprinkle with salt and paprika.

3. Select Air Fry. Set temperature to 400°F (205°C) and set time to 10 minutes. Press Start to begin preheating.

4. Once preheated, place the pan into the oven. Flip the chicken skewers halfway during the cooking.

5. When cooking is complete, the chicken should be lightly browned.

6. Meanwhile, combine the ingredients for the sauce in a small bowl. Stir to mix well.

7. Transfer the cooked chicken skewers on a large plate, then top with cilantro, sliced bell peppers, red pepper flakes. Serve with the sauce or just baste the sauce over before serving.

Sweet-and-Sour Chicken Breasts

Prep time: 15 minutes | Cook time: 15 minutes | Serves 4

- 1 cup cornstarch
- Chicken seasoning or rub, to taste
- Salt and ground black pepper, to taste
- 2 eggs
- 2 (4-ounce/ 113-g)
- boneless, skinless chicken breasts, cut into 1-inch pieces
- 1½ cups sweet-and-sour sauce
- Cooking spray

1. Spritz the perforated pan with cooking spray.

2. Combine the cornstarch, chicken seasoning, salt, and pepper in a large bowl. Stir to mix well. Whisk the eggs in a separate bowl.

3. Dredge the chicken pieces in the bowl of cornstarch mixture first, then in the bowl of whisked eggs, and then in the cornstarch mixture again.

4. Arrange the well-coated chicken pieces in the perforated pan. Spritz with cooking spray.

5. Select Air Fry. Set temperature to 360°F (182°C) and set time to 15 minutes. Press Start to begin preheating.

6. Once preheated, place the pan into the oven. Flip the chicken halfway through.

7. When cooking is complete, the chicken should be golden brown and crispy.

8. Transfer the chicken pieces on a large serving plate, then baste with sweet-and-sour sauce before serving.

Teriyaki Chicken Thighs

Prep time: 30 minutes | Cook time: 34 minutes | Serves 4

- ¼ cup chicken broth
- ½ teaspoon grated fresh ginger
- ⅛ teaspoon red pepper flakes
- 1½ tablespoons soy sauce
- 4 (5-ounce / 142-g) bone-in chicken thighs, trimmed
- 1 tablespoon mirin
- ½ teaspoon cornstarch
- 1 tablespoon sugar
- 6 ounces (170 g) snow peas, strings removed
- ⅛ teaspoon lemon zest
- 1 garlic clove, minced
- ¼ teaspoon salt
- Ground black pepper, to taste
- ½ teaspoon lemon juice

1. Combine the broth, ginger, pepper flakes, and soy sauce in a large bowl. Stir to mix well.

2. Pierce 10 to 15 holes into the chicken skin. Put the chicken in the broth mixture and toss to coat well. Let sit for 10 minutes to marinate.

3. Transfer the marinated chicken on a plate and pat dry with paper towels.

4. Scoop 2 tablespoons of marinade in a microwave-safe bowl and combine with mirin, cornstarch and sugar. Stir to mix well. Microwave for 1 minute or until frothy and has a thick consistency. Set aside.

5. Arrange the chicken in the perforated pan, skin side up.

6. Select Air Fry. Set temperature to 400°F (205°C) and set time to 25 minutes. Press Start to begin preheating.

7. Once preheated, place the pan into the oven. Flip the chicken halfway through.

8. When cooking is complete, brush the chicken skin with marinade mixture. Air fry the chicken for 5 more minutes or until glazed.

9. Remove the chicken from the oven. Allow the chicken to cool for 10 minutes.

10. Meanwhile, combine the snow peas, lemon zest, garlic, salt, and ground black pepper in a small bowl. Toss to coat well.

11. Transfer the snow peas in the perforated pan.

12. Select Air Fry. Set temperature to 400°F (205°C) and set time to 3 minutes. Place the pan into the oven.

13. When cooking is complete, the peas should be soft.

14. Remove the peas from the oven and toss with lemon juice.

15. Serve the chicken with lemony snow peas.

Five-Spice Turkey Thighs

Prep time: 10 minutes | Cook time: 25 minutes | Serves 6

- 2 pounds (907 g) turkey thighs
- 1 teaspoon Chinese five-spice powder
- ¼ teaspoon Sichuan pepper
- 1 teaspoon pink Himalayan salt
- 1 tablespoon Chinese rice vinegar
- 1 tablespoon mustard
- 1 tablespoon chili sauce
- 2 tablespoons soy sauce
- Cooking spray

1. Spritz the perforated pan with cooking spray.

2. Rub the turkey thighs with five-spice powder, Sichuan pepper, and salt on a clean work surface.

3. Put the turkey thighs in the perforated pan and spritz with cooking spray.

4. Select Air Fry. Set temperature to 360°F (182°C) and set time to 22 minutes. Press Start to begin preheating.

5. Once preheated, place the pan into the oven. Flip the thighs at least three times during the cooking.

6. When cooking is complete, the thighs should be well browned.

7. Meanwhile, heat the remaining ingredients in a saucepan over medium-high heat. Cook for 3 minutes or until the sauce is thickened and reduces to two thirds.

8. Transfer the thighs onto a plate and baste with sauce before serving.

Dijon Turkey Breast with Sage

Prep time: 5 minutes | Cook time: 30 minutes | Serves 4

- 1 teaspoon chopped fresh sage
- 1 teaspoon chopped fresh tarragon
- 1 teaspoon chopped fresh thyme leaves
- 1 teaspoon chopped fresh rosemary leaves
- 1½ teaspoons sea salt
- 1 teaspoon ground black pepper
- 1 (2-pound / 907-g) turkey breast
- 3 tablespoons Dijon mustard
- 3 tablespoons butter, melted
- Cooking spray

1. Spritz the perforated pan with cooking spray.

2. Combine the herbs, salt, and black pepper in a small bowl. Stir to mix well. Set aside.

3. Combine the Dijon mustard and butter in a separate bowl. Stir to mix well.

4. Rub the turkey with the herb mixture on a clean work surface, then brush the turkey with Dijon mixture.

5. Arrange the turkey in the perforated pan.

6. Select Air Fry. Set temperature to 390°F (199°C) and set time to 30 minutes. Press Start to begin preheating.

7. Once preheated, place the pan into the oven. Flip the turkey breast halfway through.

8. When cooking is complete, an instant-read thermometer inserted in the thickest part of the turkey breast should reach at least 165°F (74°C).

9. Transfer the cooked turkey breast on a large plate and slice to serve.

Sweet-and-Sour Drumsticks

Prep time: 5 minutes | Cook time: 23 to 25 minutes | Serves 4

- 6 chicken drumsticks
- 3 tablespoons lemon juice, divided
- 3 tablespoons low-sodium soy sauce, divided
- 1 tablespoon peanut oil
- 3 tablespoons honey
- 3 tablespoons brown sugar
- 2 tablespoons ketchup
- ¼ cup pineapple juice

1. Place the crisper tray on the bake position. Select Bake, set the temperature to 350°F (177°C), and set the time to 18 minutes.

2. Sprinkle the drumsticks with 1 tablespoon of lemon juice and 1 tablespoon of soy sauce. Place in the crisper tray and drizzle with the peanut oil. Toss to coat. Bake for 18 minutes, or until the chicken is almost done.

3. Meanwhile, in a metal bowl, combine the remaining 2 tablespoons of lemon juice, the remaining 2 tablespoons of soy sauce, honey, brown sugar, ketchup, and pineapple juice.

4. Add the cooked chicken to the bowl and stir to coat the chicken well with the sauce.

5. Place the metal bowl in the crisper tray. Bake for 5 to 7 minutes or until the chicken is glazed and registers 165°F (74°C) on a meat thermometer. Serve warm.

Roasted Chicken Tenders with Veggies

Prep time: 10 minutes | Cook time: 18 to 20 minutes | Serves 4

- 1 pound (454 g) chicken tenders
- 1 tablespoon honey
- Pinch salt
- Freshly ground black pepper, to taste
- ½ cup soft fresh bread crumbs
- ½ teaspoon dried thyme
- 1 tablespoon olive oil
- 2 carrots, sliced
- 12 small red panatoes

1. Place the crisper tray on the roast position. Select Roast, set the temperature to 380°F (193°C), and set the time to 20 minutes.

2. In a medium bowl, toss the chicken tenders with the honey, salt, and pepper.

3. In a shallow bowl, combine the bread crumbs, thyme, and olive oil, and mix.

4. Coat the tenders in the bread crumbs, pressing firmly onto the meat.

5. Place the carrots and panatoes in the crisper tray and top with the chicken tenders.

6. Roast for 18 to 20 minutes, or until the chicken is cooked to 165°F (74°C) and the vegetables are tender, shaking the crisper tray halfway during the cooking time.

7. Serve warm.

Dill Chicken Strips

Prep time: 15 minutes | Cook time: 10 minutes | Serves 4

- 2 whole boneless, skinless chicken breasts, halved lengthwise
- 1 cup Italian dressing
- 3 cups finely crushed panato chips
- 1 tablespoon dried dill weed
- 1 tablespoon garlic powder
- 1 large egg, beaten
- Cooking spray

1. In a large resealable bag, combine the chicken and Italian dressing. Seal the bag and refrigerate to marinate at least 1 hour.

2. In a shallow dish, stir together the panato chips, dill, and garlic powder. Place the beaten egg in a second shallow dish.

3. Remove the chicken from the marinade. Roll the chicken pieces in the egg and the panato chip mixture, coating thoroughly.

4. Place the baking pan on the bake position. Select Bake, set the temperature to 325°F (163°C), and set the time to 10 minutes.

5. Place the coated chicken in the baking pan and spritz with cooking spray.

6. Bake for 5 minutes. Flip the chicken, spritz it with cooking spray, and bake for 5 minutes more until the outsides are crispy and the insides are no longer pink. Serve immediately.

Honey Rosemary Chicken

Prep time: 10 minutes | Cook time: 20 minutes | Serves 4

- ¼ cup balsamic vinegar
- ¼ cup honey
- 2 tablespoons olive oil
- 1 tablespoon dried rosemary leaves
- 1 teaspoon salt
- ½ teaspoon freshly ground black pepper
- 2 whole boneless, skinless chicken breasts (about 1 pound / 454 g each), halved
- Cooking spray

1. In a large resealable bag, combine the vinegar, honey, olive oil, rosemary, salt, and pepper. Add the chicken pieces, seal

the bag, and refrigerate to marinate for at least 2 hours.

2. Place the crisper tray on the bake position. Select Bake, set the temperature to 325°F (163°C), and set the time to 20 minutes.

3. Line the crisper tray with parchment paper.

4. Remove the chicken from the marinade and place it on the parchment. Spritz with cooking spray.

5. Bake for 10 minutes. Flip the chicken, spritz it with cooking spray, and bake for 10 minutes more until the internal temperature reaches 165°F (74°C) and the chicken is no longer pink inside. Let sit for 5 minutes before serving.

Potato Cheese Crusted Chicken

Prep time: 15 minutes | Cook time: 22 to 25 minutes | Serves 4

- ¼ cup buttermilk
- 1 large egg, beaten
- 1 cup instant panato flakes
- ¼ cup grated Parmesan cheese
- 1 teaspoon salt
- ½ teaspoon freshly ground black pepper
- 2 whole boneless, skinless chicken breasts (about 1 pound / 454 g each), halved
- Cooking spray

1. Place the crisper tray on the bake position. Select Bake, set the temperature to 325°F (163°C), and set the time to 25 minutes.

2. Line the crisper tray with parchment paper.

3. In a shallow bowl, whisk the buttermilk and egg until blended. In another shallow bowl, stir together the panato flakes, cheese, salt, and pepper.

4. One at a time, dip the chicken pieces in the buttermilk mixture and the panato flake mixture, coating thoroughly.

5. Place the coated chicken on the parchment and spritz with cooking spray.

6. Bake for 15 minutes. Flip the chicken, spritz it with cooking spray, and bake for 7 to 10 minutes more until the outside is crispy and the inside is no longer pink. Serve immediately.

Blackened Chicken Breasts

Prep time: 10 minutes | Cook time: 20 minutes | Serves 4

- 1 large egg, beaten
- ¾ cup Blackened seasoning
- 2 whole boneless, skinless
- chicken breasts (about 1 pound / 454 g each), halved
- Cooking spray

1. Line the crisper tray with parchment paper.

2. Place the crisper tray on the air fry position. Select Air Fry, set the temperature to 360°F (182°C), and set the time to 20 minutes.

3. Place the beaten egg in one shallow bowl and the Blackened seasoning in another shallow bowl.

4. One at a time, dip the chicken pieces in the beaten egg and the Blackened seasoning, coating thoroughly.

5. Place the chicken pieces on the parchment and spritz with cooking spray.

6. Air fry for 10 minutes. Flip the chicken, spritz it with cooking spray, and air fry for 10 minutes more until the internal temperature reaches 165°F (74°C) and the chicken is no longer pink inside.

7. Let sit for 5 minutes before serving.

Mayonnaise-Mustard Chicken

Prep time: 10 minutes | Cook time: 15 minutes | Serves 4

- 6 tablespoons mayonnaise
- 2 tablespoons coarse-ground mustard
- 2 teaspoons honey (optional)
- 2 teaspoons curry powder
- 1 teaspoon kosher salt
- 1 teaspoon cayenne pepper
- 1 pound (454 g) chicken tenders

1. Place the crisper tray on the bake position. Select Bake, set the temperature to 350°F (177°C), and set the time to 15 minutes.

2. In a large bowl, whisk together the mayonnaise, mustard, honey (if using), curry powder, salt, and cayenne. Transfer half of the mixture to a serving bowl to serve as a dipping sauce. Add the chicken tenders to the large bowl and toss until well coated.

3. Place the tenders in the crisper tray. Bake for 15 minutes. Use a meat thermometer to ensure the chicken has reached an internal temperature of 165°F (74°C).

4. Serve the chicken with the dipping sauce.

Ginger Chicken Thighs

Prep time: 10 minutes | Cook time: 10 minutes | Serves 4

- ¼ cup julienned peeled fresh ginger
- 2 tablespoons vegetable oil
- 1 tablespoon honey
- 1 tablespoon soy sauce
- 1 tablespoon ketchup
- 1 teaspoon garam masala
- 1 teaspoon ground turmeric
- ¼ teaspoon kosher salt
- ½ teaspoon cayenne pepper
- Vegetable oil spray
- 1 pound (454 g) boneless, skinless chicken thighs, cut crosswise into thirds
- ¼ cup chopped fresh cilantro, for garnish

1. In a small bowl, combine the ginger, oil, honey, soy sauce, ketchup, garam masala, turmeric, salt, and cayenne. Whisk until well combined. Place the chicken in a resealable plastic bag and pour the marinade over. Seal the bag and massage to cover all of the chicken with the marinade. Marinate at room temperature for 30 minutes or in the

refrigerator for up to 24 hours.

2. Place the crisper tray on the bake position. Select Bake, set the temperature to 350°F (177°C), and set the time to 10 minutes.

3. Spray the crisper tray with vegetable oil spray and add the chicken and as much of the marinade and julienned ginger as possible.

4. Bake for 10 minutes. Use a meat thermometer to ensure the chicken has reached an internal temperature of 165°F (74°C).

5. To serve, garnish with cilantro.

Sweet and Spicy Turkey Meatballs

Prep time: 15 minutes | Cook time: 15 minutes | Serves 6

- 1 pound (454 g) lean ground turkey
- ½ cup whole-wheat panko bread crumbs
- 1 egg, beaten
- 1 tablespoon soy sauce
- ¼ cup plus 1 tablespoon hoisin sauce, divided
- 2 teaspoons minced garlic
- ⅛ teaspoon salt
- ⅛ teaspoon freshly ground black pepper
- 1 teaspoon sriracha
- Olive oil spray

1. Spray the crisper tray lightly with olive oil spray.

2. Place the crisper tray on the air fry position. Select Air Fry, set the temperature to 350°F (177°C), and set the time to 15 minutes.

3. In a large bowl, mix together the turkey, panko bread crumbs, egg, soy sauce, 1 tablespoon of hoisin sauce, garlic, salt, and black pepper.

4. Using a tablespoon, form the mixture into 24 meatballs.

5. In a small bowl, combine the remaining ¼ cup of hoisin sauce and sriracha to make a glaze and set aside.

6. Place the meatballs in the crisper tray in a single layer. You may need to cook them in batches.

7. Air fry for 8 minutes. Brush the meatballs generously with the glaze and air fry until cooked through, an additional 4 to 7 minutes.

8. Serve warm.

Turkey Stuffed Bell Peppers

Prep time: 20 minutes | Cook time: 15 minutes | Serves 4

- ½ pound (227 g) lean ground turkey
- 4 medium bell peppers
- 1 (15-ounce / 425-g) can black beans, drained and rinsed
- 1 cup shredded reduced-fat Cheddar cheese
- 1 cup cooked long-grain brown rice
- 1 cup mild salsa
- 1¼ teaspoons chili powder
- 1 teaspoon salt
- ½ teaspoon ground cumin
- ½ teaspoon freshly ground black pepper
- Olive oil spray
- Chopped fresh cilantro, for garnish

1. Place the crisper tray on the air fry position. Select Air Fry, set the temperature to 360°F (182°C), and set the time to 15 minutes.

2. In a large skillet over medium-high heat, cook the turkey, breaking it up with a spoon, until browned, about 5 minutes. Drain off any excess fat.

3. Cut about ½ inch off the tops of the peppers and then cut in half lengthwise. Remove and discard the seeds and set the peppers aside.

4. In a large bowl, combine the browned turkey, black beans, Cheddar cheese, rice, salsa, chili powder, salt, cumin, and black pepper. Spoon the mixture into the bell peppers.

5. Lightly spray the crisper tray with olive oil spray.

6. Place the stuffed peppers in the crisper tray. Air fry for 10 to 15 minutes until heated through.

7. Garnish with cilantro and serve.

Turkey Hoisin Burgers

Prep time: 10 minutes | Cook time: 20 minutes | Serves 4

- 1 pound (454 g) lean ground turkey
- ¼ cup whole-wheat bread crumbs
- ¼ cup hoisin sauce
- 2 tablespoons soy sauce
- 4 whole-wheat buns
- Olive oil spray

1. In a large bowl, mix together the turkey, bread crumbs, hoisin sauce, and soy sauce.

2. Form the mixture into 4 equal patties. Cover with plastic wrap and refrigerate the patties for 30 minutes.

3. Spray the crisper tray lightly with olive oil spray.

4. Place the crisper tray on the air fry position. Select Air Fry, set the temperature to 370°F (188°C), and set the time to 20 minutes.

5. Place the patties in the crisper tray in a single layer. Spray the patties lightly with olive oil spray.

6. Air fry for 10 minutes. Flip the patties over, lightly spray with olive oil spray, and air fry for an additional 5 to 10 minutes, until golden brown.

7. Place the patties on buns and top with your choice of low-calorie burger toppings like sliced tomatoes, onions, and cabbage slaw. Serve immediately.

Spiced Turkey Tenderloin

Prep time: 20 minutes | Cook time: 30 minutes | Serves 4

- ½ teaspoon paprika
- ½ teaspoon garlic powder
- ½ teaspoon salt
- ½ teaspoon freshly ground black pepper
- Pinch cayenne pepper
- 1½ pounds (680 g) turkey breast tenderloin
- Olive oil spray

1. Spray the crisper tray lightly with olive oil spray.
2. Place the crisper tray on the air fry position. Select Air Fry, set the temperature to 370°F (188°C), and set the time to 30 minutes.
3. In a small bowl, combine the paprika, garlic powder, salt, black pepper, and cayenne pepper. Rub the mixture all over the turkey.
4. Place the turkey in the crisper tray and lightly spray with olive oil spray.
5. Air fry for 15 minutes. Flip the turkey over and lightly spray with olive oil spray. air fry until the internal temperature reaches at least 170°F (77°C) for an additional 10 to 15 minutes.
6. Let the turkey rest for 10 minutes before slicing and serving.

Mini Turkey Meatloaves with Carrot

Prep time: 6 minutes | Cook time: 20 to 24 minutes | Serves 4

- ⅓ cup minced onion
- ¼ cup grated carrot
- 2 garlic cloves, minced
- 2 tablespoons ground almonds
- 2 teaspoons olive oil
- 1 teaspoon dried marjoram
- 1 egg white
- ¾ pound (340 g) ground turkey breast

1. Place the baking pan on the bake position. Select Bake, set the temperature to 400°F (204°C), and set the time to 24 minutes.
2. In a medium bowl, stir together the onion, carrot, garlic, almonds, olive oil, marjoram, and egg white.
3. Add the ground turkey. With your hands, gently but thoroughly mix until combined.
4. Double 16 foil muffin cup liners to make 8 cups. Divide the turkey mixture evenly among the liners. Transfer to the pan.
5. Bake for 20 to 24 minutes, or until the meatloaves reach an internal temperature of 165°F (74°C) on a meat thermometer. Serve immediately.

Easy Asian Turkey Meatballs

Prep time: 10 minutes | Cook time: 11 to 14 minutes | Serves 4

- 2 tablespoons peanut oil, divided
- 1 small onion, minced
- ¼ cup water chestnuts, finely chopped
- ½ teaspoon ground ginger
- 2 tablespoons low-sodium soy sauce
- ¼ cup panko bread crumbs
- 1 egg, beaten
- 1 pound (454 g) ground turkey

1. Place the baking pan on the air fry position. Select Air Fry, set the temperature to 400°F (204°C), and set the time to 2 minutes.
2. In the baking pan, combine 1 tablespoon of peanut oil and onion. Air fry for 1 to 2 minutes or until crisp and tender. Transfer the onion to a medium bowl.
3. Add the water chestnuts, ground ginger, soy sauce, and bread crumbs to the onion and mix well. Add egg and stir well. Mix in the ground turkey until combined.
4. Form the mixture into 1-inch meatballs. Drizzle the remaining 1 tablespoon of oil over the meatballs. Arrange the meatballs in the pan.
5. Bake for 10 to 12 minutes, or until they are 165°F (74°C) on a meat thermometer. Rest for 5 minutes before serving.

Dijon Turkey with Carrots

Prep time: 10 minutes | Cook time: 25 minutes | Serves 4

- 2 (12-ounce / 340-g) turkey tenderloins
- 1 teaspoon kosher salt, divided
- 6 slices bacon
- 3 tablespoons balsamic vinegar
- 2 tablespoons honey
- 1 tablespoon Dijon mustard
- ½ teaspoon dried thyme
- 6 large carrots, peeled and cut into ¼-inch rounds
- 1 tablespoon olive oil

1. Sprinkle the turkey with ¾ teaspoon of the salt. Wrap each tenderloin with 3 strips of bacon, securing the bacon with toothpicks. Place the turkey in a baking pan.
2. In a small bowl, mix the balsamic vinegar, honey, mustard, and thyme.
3. Place the carrots in a medium bowl and drizzle with the oil. Add 1 tablespoon of the balsamic mixture and ¼ teaspoon of kosher salt and toss to coat. Place these on the pan around the turkey tenderloins. Baste the tenderloins with about one-half of the remaining balsamic mixture.
4. Select Roast. Set temperature to 375°F (190°C) and set time to 25 minutes. Press Start to begin preheating.
5. Once preheated, place the pan into the oven.
6. After 13 minutes, remove the pan from the oven. Gently stir the carrots. Flip the tenderloins and baste with the remaining balsamic mixture. Return the pan to the oven and continue cooking.
7. When cooking is complete, the carrots should tender and the center of the tenderloins should register 165°F (74°C) on a meat thermometer. Remove the pan from the oven. Slice the turkey and serve with the carrots.

Chicken and Cheese Sandwiches

Prep time: 12 minutes | Cook time: 13 minutes | Serves 4

- 2 (8-ounce / 227-g) boneless, skinless chicken breasts
- 1 teaspoon kosher salt, divided
- 1 cup all-purpose flour
- 1 teaspoon Italian seasoning
- 2 large eggs
- 2 tablespoons plain yogurt
- 2 cups panko bread crumbs
- 1⅓ cups grated Parmesan cheese, divided
- 2 tablespoons olive oil
- 4 ciabatta rolls, split in half
- ½ cup marinara sauce
- ½ cup shredded Mozzarella cheese

1. Lay the chicken breasts on a cutting board and cut each one in half parallel to the board so you have 4 fairly even, flat fillets. Place a piece of plastic wrap over the chicken pieces and use a rolling pin to gently pound them to an even thickness, about ½-inch thick. Season the chicken on both sides with ½ teaspoon of kosher salt.

2. Place the flour on a plate and add the remaining kosher salt and the Italian seasoning. Mix with a fork to distribute evenly. In a wide bowl, whisk together the eggs with the yogurt. In a small bowl combine the panko, 1 cup of Parmesan cheese, and olive oil. Place this in a shallow bowl.

3. Lightly dredge both sides of the chicken pieces in the seasoned flour, and then dip them in the egg wash to coat completely, letting the excess drip off. Finally, dredge the chicken in the bread crumbs. Carefully place the breaded chicken pieces in the perforated pan.

4. Select Nuwave Air Fryer Oven. Set temperature to 375°F (190°C) and set time to 10 minutes. Press Start to begin preheating.

5. Once preheated, place the perforated pan into the oven.

6. After 5 minutes, remove the perforated pan from the oven. Carefully turn the chicken over. Return the perforated pan to the oven and continue cooking. When cooking is complete, remove the perforated pan from the oven.

7. Unfold the rolls on the perforated pan and spread each half with 1 tablespoon of marinara sauce. Place a chicken breast piece on the bottoms of the buns and sprinkle the remaining Parmesan cheese over the chicken pieces. Divide the Mozzarella among the top halves of the buns.

8. Select Broil. Set temperature to High, and set time to 3 minutes.

9. Place the pan into the oven. Check the sandwiches halfway through. When cooking is complete, the Mozzarella cheese should be melted and bubbly.

10. Remove the perforated pan from the oven. Close the sandwiches and serve.

Balsamic Chicken Breast with Oregano

Prep time: 35 minutes | Cook time: 40 minutes | Serves 2

- ¼ cup balsamic vinegar
- 2 teaspoons dried oregano
- 2 garlic cloves, minced
- 1 tablespoon olive oil
- ⅛ teaspoon salt
- ½ teaspoon freshly ground black pepper
- 2 (4-ounce / 113-g) boneless, skinless, chicken-breast halves
- Cooking spray

1. In a small bowl, add the vinegar, oregano, garlic, olive oil, salt, and pepper. Mix to combine.

2. Put the chicken in a resealable plastic bag. Pour the vinegar mixture in the bag with the chicken, seal the bag, and shake to coat the chicken. Refrigerate for 30 minutes to marinate.

3. Spritz a baking pan with cooking spray. Put the chicken in the prepared baking pan and pour the marinade over the chicken.

4. Select Bake. Set temperature to 400°F (205°C) and set time to 40 minutes. Press Start to begin preheating.

5. Once preheated, place the pan into the oven.

6. After 20 minutes, remove the pan from the oven. Flip the chicken. Return the pan to the oven and continue cooking.

7. When cooking is complete, the internal temperature of the chicken should registers at least 165°F (74°C).

8. Let sit for 5 minutes, then serve.

Chicken Kebabs with Corn Salad

Prep time: 17 minutes | Cook time: 10 minutes | Serves 4

- 1 pound (454 g) boneless, skinless chicken breast, cut into 1½-inch chunks
- 1 green bell pepper, deseeded and cut into 1-inch pieces
- 1 red bell pepper, deseeded and cut into 1-inch pieces
- 1 large onion, cut into large chunks
- 2 tablespoons fajita seasoning
- 3 tablespoons vegetable oil, divided
- 2 teaspoons kosher salt, divided
- 2 cups corn, drained
- ¼ teaspoon granulated garlic
- 1 teaspoon freshly squeezed lime juice
- 1 tablespoon mayonnaise
- 3 tablespoons grated Parmesan cheese

Special Equipment:

- 12 wooden skewers, soaked in water for at least 30 minutes

1. Place the chicken, bell peppers, and onion in a large bowl. Add the fajita seasoning, 2 tablespoons of vegetable oil, and 1½ teaspoons of kosher salt. Toss to coat evenly.

2. Alternate the chicken and vegetables on the skewers, making about 12 skewers.

3. Place the corn in a medium bowl and add the remaining vegetable oil. Add the remaining kosher salt and the garlic,

and toss to coat. Place the corn in an even layer on a baking pan and place the skewers on top.

4. Select Roast. Set temperature to 375°F (190°C) and set time to 10 minutes. Press Start to begin preheating.

5. Once preheated, place the pan into the oven.

6. After about 5 minutes, remove the pan from the oven and turn the skewers. Return the pan to the oven and continue cooking.

7. When cooking is complete, remove the pan from the oven. Place the skewers on a platter. Put the corn back to the bowl and combine with the lime juice, mayonnaise, and Parmesan cheese. Stir to mix well. Serve the skewers with the corn.

Cheddar Turkey Burgers with Mayo

Prep time: 10 minutes | Cook time: 25 minutes | Serves 4

- 2 medium yellow onions
- 1 tablespoon olive oil
- 1½ teaspoons kosher salt, divided
- 1¼ pound (567 g) ground turkey
- ⅓ cup mayonnaise
- 1 tablespoon Dijon mustard
- 2 teaspoons Worcestershire sauce
- 4 slices sharp Cheddar cheese (about 4 ounces / 113 g in total)
- 4 hamburger buns, sliced

1. Trim the onions and cut them in half through the root. Cut one of the halves in half. Grate one quarter. Place the grated onion in a large bowl. Thinly slice the remaining onions and place in a medium bowl with the oil and ½ teaspoon of kosher salt. Toss to coat. Place the onions in a single layer on a baking pan.

2. Select Roast. Set temperature to 350°F (180°C) and set time to 10 minutes. Press Start to begin preheating.

3. Once preheated, place the pan into the oven.

4. While the onions are cooking, add the turkey to the grated onion. Add the remaining kosher salt, mayonnaise, mustard, and Worcestershire sauce. Mix just until combined, being careful not to overwork the turkey. Divide the mixture into 4 patties, each about ¾-inch thick.

5. When cooking is complete, remove the pan from the oven. Move the onions to one side of the pan and place the burgers on the pan. Poke your finger into the center of each burger to make a deep indentation.

6. Select Broil. Set temperature to High, and set time to 12 minutes.

7. Place the pan into the oven. After 6 minutes, remove the pan. Turn the burgers and stir the onions. Return the pan to the oven and continue cooking. After about 4 minutes, remove the pan and place the cheese slices on the burgers. Return the pan to the oven and continue cooking for about 1 minute, or until the cheese is melted and the center of the burgers has reached at least 165°F (74°C) on a meat thermometer.

8. When cooking is complete, remove the pan from the oven. Loosely cover the burgers with foil.

9. Lay out the buns, cut-side up, on the oven rack. Select Broil. Set temperature to High, and set time to 3 minutes. Place the pan into the oven. Check the buns after 2 minutes; they should be lightly browned.

10. Remove the buns from the oven. Assemble the burgers and serve.

Curried Chicken and Brussels Sprout

Prep time: 10 minutes | Cook time: 20 minutes | Serves 4

- 1 pound (454 g) boneless, skinless chicken thighs
- 1 teaspoon kosher salt, divided
- ¼ cup unsalted butter, melted
- 1 tablespoon curry powder
- 2 medium sweet potatoes, peeled and cut in 1-inch cubes
- 12 ounces (340 g) Brussels sprouts, halved

1. Sprinkle the chicken thighs with ½ teaspoon of kosher salt. Place them in the single layer on a baking pan.

2. In a small bowl, stir together the butter and curry powder.

3. Place the sweet potatoes and Brussels sprouts in a large bowl. Drizzle half the curry butter over the vegetables and add the remaining kosher salt. Toss to coat. Transfer the vegetables to the baking pan and place in a single layer around the chicken. Brush half of the remaining curry butter over the chicken.

4. Select Roast. Set temperature to 400°F (205°C) and set time to 20 minutes. Press Start to begin preheating.

5. Once preheated, place the pan into the oven.

6. After 10 minutes, remove the pan from the oven and turn over the chicken thighs. Baste them with the remaining curry butter. Return the pan to the oven and continue cooking.

7. Cooking is complete when the sweet potatoes are tender and the chicken is cooked through and reads 165°F (74°C) on a meat thermometer.

Chicken and Ham Rochambeau

Prep time: 25 minutes | Cook time: 30 minutes | Serves 4

- 1 tablespoon melted butter
- ¼ cup all-purpose flour
- 4 chicken tenders, cut in half crosswise
- 4 slices ham, ¼-inch thick, large enough to cover an English muffin
- 2 English muffins, split in
- halves
- Salt and ground black pepper, to taste
- Cooking spray

Mushroom Sauce:
- 2 tablespoons butter
- ½ cup chopped

- mushrooms
- ½ cup chopped green onions
- 2 tablespoons flour
- 1 cup chicken broth
- 1½ teaspoons Worcestershire sauce
- ¼ teaspoon garlic powder

1. Put the butter in a baking pan. Combine the flour, salt, and ground black pepper in a shallow dish. Roll the chicken tenders over to coat well.
2. Arrange the chicken in the baking pan and flip to coat with the melted butter.
3. Select Broil. Set temperature to 390°F (199°C) and set time to 10 minutes. Press Start to begin preheating.
4. Once preheated, place the pan into the oven. Flip the tenders halfway through.
5. When cooking is complete, the juices of chicken tenders should run clear.
6. Meanwhile, make the mushroom sauce: melt 2 tablespoons of butter in a saucepan over medium-high heat.
7. Add the mushrooms and onions to the saucepan and sauté for 3 minutes or until the onions are translucent.
8. Gently mix in the flour, broth, Worcestershire sauce, and garlic powder until smooth.
9. Reduce the heat to low and simmer for 5 minutes or until it has a thick consistency. Set the sauce aside until ready to serve.
10. When broiling is complete, remove the baking pan from the oven and set the ham slices into the perforated pan.
11. Select Nuwave Air Fryer Oven. Set time to 5 minutes. Flip the ham slices halfway through.
12. When cooking is complete, the ham slices should be heated through.
13. Remove the ham slices from the oven and set in the English muffin halves and warm for 1 minute.
14. Arrange each ham slice on top of each muffin half, then place each chicken tender over the ham slice.
15. Transfer to the oven and set time to 2 minutes on Nuwave Air Fryer Oven.
16. Serve with the sauce on top.

Breaded Chicken Fingers

Prep time: 20 minutes | Cook time: 10 minutes | Makes 12 chicken fingers

- ½ cup all-purpose flour
- 2 cups panko bread crumbs
- 2 tablespoons canola oil
- 1 large egg
- 3 boneless and skinless chicken breasts, each cut into 4 strips
- Kosher salt and freshly ground black pepper, to taste

- Cooking spray

1. Spritz the perforated pan with cooking spray.
2. Pour the flour in a large bowl. Combine the panko and canola oil on a shallow dish. Whisk the egg in a separate bowl.
3. Rub the chicken strips with salt and ground black pepper on a clean work surface, then dip the chicken in the bowl of flour. Shake the excess off and dunk the chicken strips in the bowl of whisked egg, then roll the strips over the panko to coat well.
4. Arrange the strips in the perforated pan.
5. Select Nuwave Air Fryer Oven. Set temperature to 360°F (182°C) and set time to 10 minutes. Press Start to begin preheating.
6. Once preheated, place the pan into the oven. Flip the strips halfway through.
7. When cooking is complete, the strips should be crunchy and lightly browned.
8. Serve immediately.

Breaded Chicken Livers

Prep time: 10 minutes | Cook time: 10 minutes | Serves 4

- 2 eggs
- 2 tablespoons water
- ¾ cup flour
- 2 cups panko bread crumbs
- 1 teaspoon salt
- ½ teaspoon ground black pepper
- 20 ounces (567 g) chicken livers
- Cooking spray

1. Spritz the perforated pan with cooking spray.
2. Whisk the eggs with water in a large bowl. Pour the flour in a separate bowl. Pour the panko on a shallow dish and sprinkle with salt and pepper.
3. Dredge the chicken livers in the flour. Shake the excess off, then dunk the livers in the whisked eggs, and then roll the livers over the panko to coat well.
4. Arrange the livers in the perforated pan and spritz with cooking spray.
5. Select Nuwave Air Fryer Oven. Set temperature to 390°F (199°C) and set time to 10 minutes. Press Start to begin preheating.
6. Once preheated, place the pan into the oven. Flip the livers halfway through.
7. When cooking is complete, the livers should be golden and crispy.
8. Serve immediately.

Breaded Chicken Tenders with Thyme

Prep time: 15 minutes | Cook time: 5 minutes | Serves 4

- ½ cup all-purpose flour
- 1 teaspoon marjoram
- ½ teaspoon thyme
- 1 teaspoon dried parsley flakes
- ½ teaspoon salt
- 1 egg
- 1 teaspoon lemon juice
- 1 teaspoon water
- 1 cup bread crumbs
- 4 chicken tenders, pounded thin, cut in half lengthwise
- Cooking spray

1. Spritz the perforated pan with cooking spray.

2. Combine the flour, marjoram, thyme, parsley, and salt in a shallow dish. Stir to mix well.

3. Whisk the egg with lemon juice and water in a large bowl. Pour the bread crumbs in a separate shallow dish.

4. Roll the chicken halves in the flour mixture first, then in the egg mixture, and then roll over the bread crumbs to coat well. Shake the excess off.

5. Arrange the chicken halves in the perforated pan and spritz with cooking spray on both sides.

6. Select Nuwave Air Fryer Oven. Set temperature to 390°F (199°C) and set time to 5 minutes. Press Start to begin preheating.

7. Once preheated, place the pan into the oven. Flip the halves halfway through.

8. When cooking is complete, the chicken halves should be golden brown and crispy.

9. Serve immediately.

Chapter 3 Fish and Seafood

Lemon Red Snapper with Thyme

Prep time: 13 minutes | Cook time: 10 minutes | Serves 4

- 1 teaspoon olive oil
- 1½ teaspoons black pepper
- ¼ teaspoon garlic powder
- ¼ teaspoon thyme
- ⅛ teaspoon cayenne
- pepper
- 4 (4-ounce / 113-g) red snapper fillets, skin on
- 4 thin slices lemon
- Nonstick cooking spray

1. Spritz the perforated pan with nonstick cooking spray.
2. In a small bowl, stir together the olive oil, black pepper, garlic powder, thyme, and cayenne pepper. Rub the mixture all over the fillets until completely coated.
3. Lay the fillets, skin-side down, in the perforated pan and top each fillet with a slice of lemon.
4. Select Bake. Set temperature to 390°F (199°C) and set time to 10 minutes. Press Start to begin preheating.
5. Once preheated, place the pan into the oven. Flip the fillets halfway through.
6. When cooking is complete, the fish should be cooked through. Let the fish cool for 5 minutes and serve.

Snapper Fillets with Capers

Prep time: 9 minutes | Cook time: 18 minutes | Serves 4

- 2 tablespoons extra-virgin olive oil
- 2 large garlic cloves, minced
- ½ onion, finely chopped
- 1 (14.5-ounce / 411-g) can diced tomatoes, drained
- ¼ cup sliced green olives
- 3 tablespoons capers, divided
- 2 tablespoons chopped fresh parsley, divided
- ½ teaspoon dried oregano
- 4 (6-ounce / 170-g) snapper fillets
- ½ teaspoon kosher salt

1. Grease the sheet pan generously with olive oil, then place the pan into the oven.
2. Select Roast. Set temperature to 375°F (190°C) and set time to 18 minutes. Press Start to begin preheating.
3. When the oven has preheated, remove the pan and add the garlic and onion to the olive oil in the pan, stirring to coat. Return the pan to the oven and continue cooking.
4. After 2 minutes, remove the pan from the oven. Stir in the tomatoes, olives, 1½ tablespoons of capers, 1 tablespoon of parsley, and oregano. Return the pan to the oven and continue cooking for 6 minutes until heated through.
5. Meanwhile, rub the fillets with the salt on both sides.
6. After another 6 minutes, remove the pan. Put the fillets in the center of the sheet pan and spoon some of the sauce over them. Return the pan to the oven and continue cooking, or until the fish is flaky.
7. When cooked, remove the pan from the oven. Scatter the remaining 1½ tablespoons of capers and 1 tablespoon of parsley on top of the fillets, then serve.

Salmon and Pepper Bowl

Prep time: 115 minutes | Cook time: 12 minutes | Serves 4

- 12 ounces (340 g) salmon fillets, cut into 1½-inch cubes
- 1 red onion, chopped
- 1 jalapeño pepper, minced
- 1 red bell pepper, chopped
- ¼ cup low-sodium salsa
- 2 teaspoons peanut oil or safflower oil
- 2 tablespoons low-sodium tomato juice
- 1 teaspoon chili powder

1. Mix together the salmon cubes, red onion, jalapeño, red bell pepper, salsa, peanut oil, tomato juice, chili powder in a medium metal bowl and stir until well incorporated.
2. Select Bake. Set temperature to 370°F (188°C) and set time to 12 minutes. Press Start to begin preheating.
3. Once preheated, place the metal bowl into the oven. Stir the ingredients once halfway through the cooking time.
4. When cooking is complete, the salmon should be cooked through and the veggies should be fork-tender. Serve warm.

Curried Halibut Fillets with Parmesan

Prep time: 5 minutes | Cook time: 10 minutes | Serves 4

- 2 medium-sized halibut fillets
- Dash of tabasco sauce
- 1 teaspoon curry powder
- ½ teaspoon ground coriander
- ½ teaspoon hot paprika
- Kosher salt and freshly cracked mixed peppercorns, to taste
- 2 eggs
- 1½ tablespoons olive oil
- ½ cup grated Parmesan cheese

1. On a clean work surface, drizzle the halibut fillets with the tabasco sauce. Sprinkle with the curry powder, coriander, hot paprika, salt, and cracked mixed peppercorns. Set aside.
2. In a shallow bowl, beat the eggs until frothy. In another shallow bowl, combine the olive oil and Parmesan cheese.
3. One at a time, dredge the halibut fillets in the beaten eggs, shaking off any excess, then roll them over the Parmesan cheese until evenly coated.
4. Arrange the halibut fillets in the perforated pan in a single layer.
5. Select Roast. Set temperature to 365°F (185°C) and set time to 10 minutes. Press Start to begin preheating.
6. Once preheated, place the pan into the oven.
7. When cooking is complete, the fish should be golden brown and crisp. Cool for 5 minutes before serving.

Cajun Cod Fillets with Lemon Pepper

Prep time: 5 minutes | Cook time: 12 minutes | Makes 2 cod fillets

- 1 tablespoon Cajun seasoning
- 1 teaspoon salt
- ½ teaspoon lemon pepper
- ½ teaspoon freshly ground black pepper
- 2 (8-ounce / 227-g) cod
- fillets, cut to fit into the perforated pan
- Cooking spray
- 2 tablespoons unsalted butter, melted
- 1 lemon, cut into 4 wedges

1. Spritz the perforated pan with cooking spray.
2. Thoroughly combine the Cajun seasoning, salt, lemon pepper, and black pepper in a small bowl. Rub this mixture all over the cod fillets until completely coated.
3. Put the fillets in the perforated pan and brush the melted butter over both sides of each fillet.
4. Select Bake. Set temperature to 360°F (182°C) and set time to 12 minutes. Press Start to begin preheating.
5. Once preheated, place the pan into the oven. Flip the fillets halfway through the cooking time.
6. When cooking is complete, the fish should flake apart with a fork. Remove the fillets from the oven and serve with fresh lemon wedges.

Garlic-Lemon Tilapia

Prep time: 5 minutes | Cook time: 10 to 15 minutes | Serves 4

- 1 tablespoon lemon juice
- 1 tablespoon olive oil
- 1 teaspoon minced garlic
- ½ teaspoon chili powder
- 4 (6-ounce / 170-g) tilapia fillets

1. Place the crisper tray on the air fry position. Select Air Fry, set the temperature to 380°F (193°C), and set the time to 15 minutes.
2. Line the crisper tray with parchment paper.
3. In a large, shallow bowl, mix together the lemon juice, olive oil, garlic, and chili powder to make a marinade. Place the tilapia fillets in the bowl and coat evenly.
4. Place the fillets in the crisper tray in a single layer, leaving space between each fillet. You may need to cook in more than one batch.
5. Air fry for 10 to 15 minutes until the fish is cooked and flakes easily with a fork.
6. Serve hot.

Cajun-Style Fish Tacos

Prep time: 5 minutes | Cook time: 10 to 15 minutes | Serves 6

- 2 teaspoons avocado oil
- 1 tablespoon Cajun seasoning
- 4 tilapia fillets
- 1 (14-ounce / 397-g) package coleslaw mix

- 12 corn tortillas
- 2 limes, cut into wedges

1. Place the crisper tray on the air fry position. Select Air Fry, set the temperature to 380°F (193°C), and set the time to 15 minutes.

2. Line the crisper tray with parchment paper.

3. In a medium, shallow bowl, mix the avocado oil and the Cajun seasoning to make a marinade. Add the tilapia fillets and coat evenly.

4. Place the fillets in the crisper tray in a single layer, leaving room between each fillet. You may need to cook in batches.

5. Air fry for 10 to 15 minutes until the fish is cooked and easily flakes with a fork.

6. Assemble the tacos by placing some of the coleslaw mix in each tortilla. Add ⅓ of a tilapia fillet to each tortilla. Squeeze some lime juice over the top of each taco and serve.

Crispy Catfish Strips

Prep time: 5 minutes | Cook time: 16 to 18 minutes | Serves 4

- 1 cup buttermilk
- 1 cup cornmeal
- 5 catfish fillets, cut into 1½-inch strips
- 1 tablespoon Creole, Cajun, or Old Bay seasoning
- Cooking spray

1. Pour the buttermilk into a shallow baking pan. Place the catfish in the dish and refrigerate for at least 1 hour to help remove any fishy taste.

2. Place the crisper tray on the air fry position. Select Air Fry, set the temperature to 400°F (204°C), and set the time to 18 minutes.

3. Spray the crisper tray lightly with cooking spray.

4. In a shallow bowl, combine cornmeal and Creole seasoning.

5. Shake any excess buttermilk off the catfish. Place each strip in the cornmeal mixture and coat completely. Press the cornmeal into the catfish gently to help it stick.

6. Place the strips in the crisper tray in a single layer. Lightly spray the catfish with cooking spray. You may need to cook the catfish in more than one batch.

7. Air fry for 8 minutes. Turn the catfish strips over and lightly spray with cooking spray. air fry until golden brown and crispy, for 8 to 10 more minutes.

8. Serve warm.

Cajun-Style Salmon Burgers

Prep time: 10 minutes | Cook time: 10 to 15 minutes | Serves 4

- 4 (5-ounce / 142-g) cans pink salmon in water, any skin and bones removed, drained
- 2 eggs, beaten

- 1 cup whole-wheat bread crumbs
- 4 tablespoons light mayonnaise
- 2 teaspoons Cajun
- seasoning
- 2 teaspoons dry mustard
- 4 whole-wheat buns
- Cooking spray

1. In a medium bowl, mix the salmon, egg, bread crumbs, mayonnaise, Cajun seasoning, and dry mustard. Cover with plastic wrap and refrigerate for 30 minutes.

2. Place the crisper tray on the air fry position. Select Air Fry, set the temperature to 360°F (182°C), and set the time to 15 minutes.

3. Spray the crisper tray lightly with cooking spray.

4. Shape the mixture into four ½-inch-thick patties about the same size as the buns.

5. Place the salmon patties in the crisper tray in a single layer and lightly spray the tops with cooking spray. You may need to cook them in batches.

6. Air fry for 6 to 8 minutes. Turn the patties over and lightly spray with cooking spray. air fry until crispy on the outside, for 4 to 7 more minutes.

7. Serve on whole-wheat buns.

Simple Salmon Patty Bites

Prep time: 15 minutes | Cook time: 10 to 15 minutes | Serves 4

- 4 (5-ounce / 142-g) cans pink salmon, skinless, boneless in water, drained
- 2 eggs, beaten
- 1 cup whole-wheat panko bread crumbs
- 4 tablespoons finely
- minced red bell pepper
- 2 tablespoons parsley flakes
- 2 teaspoons Old Bay seasoning
- Cooking spray

1. Place the crisper tray on the air fry position. Select Air Fry, set the temperature to 360°F (182°C), and set the time to 15 minutes.

2. Spray the crisper tray lightly with cooking spray.

3. In a medium bowl, mix the salmon, eggs, panko bread crumbs, red bell pepper, parsley flakes, and Old Bay seasoning.

4. Using a small cookie scoop, form the mixture into 20 balls.

5. Place the salmon bites in the crisper tray in a single layer and spray lightly with cooking spray. You may need to cook them in batches.

6. Air fry for 10 to 15 minutes until crispy, shaking the crisper tray a couple of times for even cooking.

7. Serve immediately.

Vegetable and Fish Tacos

Prep time: 10 minutes | Cook time: 9 to 12 minutes | Serves 4

- 1 pound (454 g) white fish fillets
- 2 teaspoons olive oil
- 3 tablespoons freshly squeezed lemon juice, divided
- 1½ cups chopped red

- cabbage
- 1 large carrot, grated
- ½ cup low-sodium salsa
- ⅓ cup low-fat Greek yogurt
- 4 soft low-sodium whole-wheat tortillas

1. Place the crisper tray on the air fry position. Select Air Fry, set the temperature to 400°F (204°C), and set the time to 12 minutes.
2. Brush the fish with the olive oil and sprinkle with 1 tablespoon of lemon juice. Air fry for 9 to 12 minutes, or until the fish just flakes when tested with a fork.
3. Meanwhile, in a medium bowl, stir together the remaining 2 tablespoons of lemon juice, the red cabbage, carrot, salsa, and yogurt.
4. When the fish is cooked, remove it from the crisper tray and break it up into large pieces.
5. Offer the fish, tortillas, and the cabbage mixture, and let each person assemble a taco.
6. Serve immediately.

Green Curry Shrimp

Prep time: 15 minutes | Cook time: 5 minutes | Serves 4

- 1 to 2 tablespoons Thai green curry paste
- 2 tablespoons coconut oil, melted
- 1 tablespoon half-and-half or coconut milk
- 1 teaspoon fish sauce
- 1 teaspoon soy sauce
- 1 teaspoon minced fresh

- ginger
- 1 clove garlic, minced
- 1 pound (454 g) jumbo raw shrimp, peeled and deveined
- ¼ cup chopped fresh Thai basil or sweet basil
- ¼ cup chopped fresh cilantro

1. In the baking pan, combine the curry paste, coconut oil, half-and-half, fish sauce, soy sauce, ginger, and garlic. Whisk until well combined.
2. Add the shrimp and toss until well coated. Marinate at room temperature for 15 to 30 minutes.
3. Place the crisper tray on the air fry position. Select Air Fry, set the temperature to 400°F (204°C), and set the time to 5 minutes.
4. Air fry for 5 minutes, stirring halfway through the cooking time.
5. Transfer the shrimp to a serving bowl or platter. Garnish with the basil and cilantro. Serve immediately.

Crispy Cod Cakes with Salad Greens

Prep time: 15 minutes | Cook time: 12 minutes | Serves 4

- 1 pound (454 g) cod fillets, cut into chunks
- ⅓ cup packed fresh basil leaves
- 3 cloves garlic, crushed
- ½ teaspoon smoked paprika
- ¼ teaspoon salt
- ¼ teaspoon pepper
- 1 large egg, beaten
- 1 cup panko bread crumbs
- Cooking spray
- Salad greens, for serving

1. In a food processor, pulse cod, basil, garlic, smoked paprika, salt, and pepper until cod is finely chopped, stirring occasionally. Form into 8 patties, about 2 inches in diameter. Dip each first into the egg, then into the panko, patting to adhere. Spray with oil on one side.
2. Place the crisper tray on the air fry position. Select Air Fry, set the temperature to 400°F (204°C), and set the time to 12 minutes.
3. Working in batches, place half the cakes in the crisper tray, oil-side down; spray with oil. Air fry for 12 minutes, until golden brown and cooked through.
4. Serve cod cakes with salad greens.

Roasted Cod with Sesame Seeds

Prep time: 5 minutes | Cook time: 7 to 9 minutes | Makes 1 fillet

- 1 tablespoon reduced-sodium soy sauce
- 2 teaspoons honey
- Cooking spray
- 6 ounces (170 g) fresh cod fillet
- 1 teaspoon sesame seeds

1. Place the crisper tray on the roast position. Select Roast, set the temperature to 360°F (182°C), and set the time to 10 minutes.
2. In a small bowl, combine the soy sauce and honey.
3. Spray the crisper tray with cooking spray, then place the cod in the crisper tray, brush with the soy mixture, and sprinkle sesame seeds on top.
4. Roast for 7 to 9 minutes, or until opaque.
5. Remove the fish and allow to cool on a wire rack for 5 minutes before serving.

Baked Flounder Fillets

Prep time: 8 minutes | Cook time: 12 minutes | Serves 2

- 2 flounder fillets, patted dry
- 1 egg
- ½ teaspoon Worcestershire sauce
- ¼ cup almond flour
- ¼ cup coconut flour
- ½ teaspoon coarse sea salt
- ½ teaspoon lemon pepper
- ¼ teaspoon chili powder
- Cooking spray

1. Place the crisper tray on the bake position. Select Bake,

set the temperature to 390°F (199°C), and set the time to 12 minutes.

2. Spritz the crisper tray with cooking spray.

3. In a shallow bowl, beat together the egg with Worcestershire sauce until well incorporated.

4. In another bowl, thoroughly combine the almond flour, coconut flour, sea salt, lemon pepper, and chili powder.

5. Dredge the fillets in the egg mixture, shaking off any excess, then roll in the flour mixture to coat well.

6. Place the fillets in the crisper tray. Bake for 7 minutes. Flip the fillets and spray with cooking spray. Continue cooking for 5 minutes, or until the fish is flaky.

7. Serve warm.

Coconut Chili Fish Curry

Prep time: 10 minutes | Cook time: 20 to 22 minutes | Serves 4

- 2 tablespoons sunflower oil, divided
- 1 pound (454 g) fish, chopped
- 1 ripe tomato, puréed
- 2 red chilies, chopped
- 1 shallot, minced
- 1 garlic clove, minced
- 1 cup coconut milk
- 1 tablespoon coriander powder
- 1 teaspoon red curry paste
- ½ teaspoon fenugreek seeds
- Salt and white pepper, to taste

1. Place the crisper tray on the air fry position. Select Air Fry, set the temperature to 380°F (193°C), and set the time to 10 minutes.

2. Coat the crisper tray with 1 tablespoon of sunflower oil.

3. Place the fish in the crisper tray. Air fry for 10 minutes. Flip the fish halfway through the cooking time.

4. When done, transfer the cooked fish to the baking pan greased with the remaining 1 tablespoon of sunflower oil. Stir in the remaining ingredients and return to the grill.

5. Reduce the temperature to 350°F (177°C) and air fry for another 10 to 12 minutes until heated through.

6. Cool for 5 to 8 minutes before serving.

Piri-Piri King Prawn

Prep time: 10 minutes | Cook time: 8 minutes | Serves 2

- 12 king prawns, rinsed
- 1 tablespoon coconut oil
- Salt and ground black pepper, to taste
- 1 teaspoon onion powder
- 1 teaspoon garlic paste
- 1 teaspoon curry powder
- ½ teaspoon piri piri powder
- ½ teaspoon cumin powder

1. Place the crisper tray on the air fry position. Select Air Fry, set the temperature to 360°F (182°C), and set the time to 8 minutes.

2. Combine all the ingredients in a large bowl and toss until the prawns are completely coated.

3. Place the prawns in the crisper tray. Air fry for 8 minutes, shaking the crisper tray halfway through, or until the prawns turn pink.

4. Serve hot.

Garlic Shrimp with Parsley

Prep time: 10 minutes | Cook time: 5 minutes | Serves 4

- 18 shrimp, shelled and deveined
- 2 garlic cloves, peeled and minced
- 2 tablespoons extra-virgin olive oil
- 2 tablespoons freshly squeezed lemon juice
- ½ cup fresh parsley,
- coarsely chopped
- 1 teaspoon onion powder
- 1 teaspoon lemon-pepper seasoning
- ½ teaspoon hot paprika
- ½ teaspoon salt
- ¼ teaspoon cumin powder

1. Toss all the ingredients in a mixing bowl until the shrimp are well coated.

2. Cover and allow to marinate in the refrigerator for 30 minutes.

3. Place the crisper tray on the air fry position. Select Air Fry, set the temperature to 400°F (204°C), and set the time to 5 minutes.

4. Arrange the shrimp in the crisper tray. Air fry for 5 minutes, or until the shrimp are pink on the outside and opaque in the center.

5. Remove from the crisper tray and serve warm.

Paprika Shrimp

Prep time: 5 minutes | Cook time: 10 minutes | Serves 4

- 1 pound (454 g) tiger shrimp
- 2 tablespoons olive oil
- ½ tablespoon old bay seasoning
- ¼ tablespoon smoked paprika
- ¼ teaspoon cayenne pepper
- A pinch of sea salt

1. Place the crisper tray on the air fry position. Select Air Fry, set the temperature to 380°F (193°C), and set the time to 10 minutes.

2. Toss all the ingredients in a large bowl until the shrimp are evenly coated.

3. Arrange the shrimp in the crisper tray. Air fry for 10 minutes, shaking the crisper tray halfway through, or until the shrimp are pink and cooked through.

4. Serve hot.

Fish and Seafood

Chapter 4 Wraps and Sandwiches

Cheesy Greens Sandwich

Prep time: 15 minutes | Cook time: 10 to 13 minutes | Serves 4

- 1½ cups chopped mixed greens
- 2 garlic cloves, thinly sliced
- 2 teaspoons olive oil
- 2 slices low-sodium low-fat Swiss cheese
- 4 slices low-sodium whole-wheat bread
- Cooking spray

1. Place the baking pan on the air fry position. Select Air Fry, set the temperature to 400°F (204°C), and set the time to 5 minutes.

2. In the baking pan, mix the greens, garlic, and olive oil. Air fry for 4 to 5 minutes, stirring once, until the vegetables are tender. Drain, if necessary.

3. Make 2 sandwiches, dividing half of the greens and 1 slice of Swiss cheese between 2 slices of bread. Lightly spray the outsides of the sandwiches with cooking spray. Transfer to the pan.

4. Bake for 6 to 8 minutes, turning with tongs halfway through, until the bread is toasted and the cheese melts.

5. Cut each sandwich in half and serve.

Veggie Pita Sandwich

Prep time: 10 minutes | Cook time: 9 to 12 minutes | Serves 4

- 1 baby eggplant, peeled   and chopped
- 1 red bell pepper, sliced
- ½ cup diced red onion
- ½ cup shredded carrot
- 1 teaspoon olive oil
- ⅓ cup low-fat Greek yogurt
- ½ teaspoon dried tarragon
- 2 low-sodium whole-wheat pita breads, halved crosswise

1. Place the baking pan on the roast position. Select Roast, set the temperature to 390°F (199°C), and set the time to 10 minutes.

2. In the pan, stir together the eggplant, red bell pepper, red onion, carrot, and olive oil. Roast for 7 to 9 minutes, stirring once, until the vegetables are tender. Drain if necessary.

3. In a small bowl, thoroughly mix the yogurt and tarragon until well combined.

4. Stir the yogurt mixture into the vegetables. Stuff one-fourth of this mixture into each pita pocket.

5. Place the sandwiches in the baking pan. Bake for 2 to 3 minutes, or until the bread is toasted.

6. Serve immediately.

Bacon and Bell Pepper Sandwich

Prep time: 10 minutes | Cook time: 6 minutes | Serves 4

- ⅓ cup spicy barbecue sauce
- 2 tablespoons honey
- 8 slices cooked bacon, cut into thirds
- 1 red bell pepper, sliced
- 1 yellow bell pepper, sliced
- 3 pita pockets, cut in half
- 1¼ cups torn butter lettuce leaves

- 2 tomatoes, sliced

1. Place the crisper tray on the roast position. Select Roast, set the temperature to 350°F (177°C), and set the time to 6 minutes.

2. In a small bowl, combine the barbecue sauce and the honey. Brush this mixture lightly onto the bacon slices and the red and yellow pepper slices.

3. Put the peppers into the crisper tray. Roast for 4 minutes. Then shake the crisper tray, add the bacon, and roast for 2 minutes or until the bacon is browned and the peppers are tender.

4. Fill the pita halves with the bacon, peppers, any remaining barbecue sauce, lettuce, and tomatoes, and serve immediately.

Tuna Muffin Sandwich

Prep time: 8 minutes | Cook time: 4 to 8 minutes | Serves 4

- 1 (6-ounce / 170-g) can chunk light tuna, drained
- ¼ cup mayonnaise
- 2 tablespoons mustard
- 1 tablespoon lemon juice
- 2 green onions, minced
- 3 English muffins, split with a fork
- 3 tablespoons softened butter
- 6 thin slices Provolone or Muenster cheese

1. Place the baking pan on the bake position. Select Bake, set the temperature to 390°F (199°C), and set the time to 4 minutes.

2. In a small bowl, combine the tuna, mayonnaise, mustard, lemon juice, and green onions. Set aside.

3. Butter the cut side of the English muffins. Place in the baking pan, butter-side up.

4. Bake for 2 to 4 minutes, or until light golden brown. Remove the muffins from the grill.

5. Top each muffin with one slice of cheese and return to the grill. Bake for 2 to 4 minutes or until the cheese melts and starts to brown.

6. Remove the muffins from the grill, top with the tuna mixture, and serve.

Cheesy Shrimp Sandwich

Prep time: 10 minutes | Cook time: 5 to 7 minutes | Serves 4

- 1¼ cups shredded Colby, Cheddar, or Havarti cheese
- 1 (6-ounce / 170-g) can tiny shrimp, drained
- 3 tablespoons mayonnaise
- 2 tablespoons minced
- green onion
- 4 slices whole grain or whole-wheat bread
- 2 tablespoons softened butter

1. Place the crisper tray on the air fry position. Select Air Fry, set the temperature to 400°F (204°C), and set the time to 7 minutes.

2. In a medium bowl, combine the cheese, shrimp, mayonnaise, and green onion, and mix well.

3. Spread this mixture on two of the slices of bread. Top with the other slices of bread to make two sandwiches. Spread the sandwiches lightly with butter. Transfer to the crisper tray.

4. Air fry for 5 to 7 minutes, or until the bread is browned and crisp and the cheese is melted.

5. Cut in half and serve warm.

Chicken Pita Sandwich

Prep time: 10 minutes | Cook time: 9 to 11 minutes | Serves 4

- 2 boneless, skinless chicken breasts, cut into 1-inch cubes
- 1 small red onion, sliced
- 1 red bell pepper, sliced
- ⅓ cup Italian salad dressing, divided
- ½ teaspoon dried thyme
- 4 pita pockets, split
- 2 cups torn butter lettuce
- 1 cup chopped cherry tomatoes

1. Place the crisper tray on the bake position. Select Bake, set the temperature to 380°F (193°C), and set the time to 11 minutes.

2. Place the chicken, onion, and bell pepper in the crisper tray. Drizzle with 1 tablespoon of the Italian salad dressing, add the thyme, and toss.

3. Bake for 9 to 11 minutes, or until the chicken is 165°F (74°C) on a food thermometer, stirring once during cooking time.

4. Transfer the chicken and vegetables to a bowl and toss with the remaining salad dressing.

5. Assemble sandwiches with the pita pockets, butter lettuce, and cherry tomatoes. Serve immediately.

Classic Sloppy Joes

Prep time: 10 minutes | Cook time: 17 to 19 minutes | Makes 4 large sandwiches or 8 sliders

- 1 pound (454 g) very lean ground beef
- 1 teaspoon onion powder
- ⅓ cup ketchup
- ¼ cup water
- ½ teaspoon celery seed
- 1 tablespoon lemon juice
- 1½ teaspoons brown sugar
- 1¼ teaspoons low-sodium Worcestershire sauce
- ½ teaspoon salt (optional)
- ½ teaspoon vinegar
- ⅛ teaspoon dry mustard
- Hamburger or slider buns, for serving
- Cooking spray

1. Place the crisper tray on the roast position. Select Roast, set the temperature to 390°F (199°C), and set the time to 12 minutes.

2. Spray the crisper tray with cooking spray.

3. Break raw ground beef into small chunks and pile into the crisper tray. Roast for 5 minutes. Stir to break apart and roast for 3 minutes. Stir and roast for 2 to 4 minutes longer, or until meat is well done.

4. Remove the meat from the grill, drain, and use a knife and fork to crumble into small pieces.

5. Give your crisper tray a quick rinse to remove any bits of meat.

6. Place all the remaining ingredients, except for the buns, in the baking pan and mix together. Add the meat and stir well.

7. Adjust the temperature to 330°F (166°C). Bake for 5 minutes. Stir and bake for 2 minutes.

8. Scoop into buns. Serve hot.

Chicken and Yogurt Taquitos

Prep time: 15 minutes | Cook time: 12 minutes | Serves 4

- 1 cup cooked chicken, shredded
- ¼ cup Greek yogurt
- ¼ cup salsa
- 1 cup shredded Mozzarella
- cheese
- Salt and ground black pepper, to taste
- 4 flour tortillas
- Cooking spray

1. Spritz the crisper tray with cooking spray.

2. Place the crisper tray on the air fry position. Select Air Fry, set the temperature to 380°F (193°C), and set the time to 12 minutes.

3. Combine all the ingredients, except for the tortillas, in a large bowl. Stir to mix well.

4. Make the taquitos: Unfold the tortillas on a clean work surface, then scoop up 2 tablespoons of the chicken mixture in the middle of each tortilla. Roll the tortillas up to wrap the filling.

5. Arrange the taquitos in the crisper tray and spritz with cooking spray.

6. Air fry for 12 minutes or until golden brown and the cheese melts. Flip the taquitos halfway through.

7. Serve immediately.

Cream Cheese Wontons

Prep time: 5 minutes | Cook time: 6 minutes | Serves 4

- 2 ounces (57 g) cream cheese, softened
- 1 tablespoon sugar
- 16 square wonton wrappers
- Cooking spray

1. Spritz the crisper tray with cooking spray.

2. Place the crisper tray on the air fry position. Select Air Fry, set the temperature to 350°F (177°C), and set the time to 6

minutes.

3. In a mixing bowl, stir together the cream cheese and sugar until well mixed. Prepare a small bowl of water alongside.

4. On a clean work surface, lay the wonton wrappers. Scoop ¼ teaspoon of cream cheese in the center of each wonton wrapper. Dab the water over the wrapper edges. Fold each wonton wrapper diagonally in half over the filling to form a triangle.

5. Arrange the wontons in the crisper tray. Spritz the wontons with cooking spray. Air fry for 6 minutes, or until golden brown and crispy. Flip once halfway through to ensure even cooking.

6. Divide the wontons among four plates. Let rest for 5 minutes before serving.

Sweet Potato and Black Bean Burritos

Prep time: 15 minutes | Cook time: 1 hour | Makes 6 burritos

- 2 sweet panatoes, peeled and cut into a small dice
- 1 tablespoon vegetable oil
- Kosher salt and ground black pepper, to taste
- 6 large flour tortillas
- 1 (16-ounce / 454-g) can refried black beans, divided
- 1½ cups baby spinach, divided
- 6 eggs, scrambled
- ¾ cup grated Cheddar cheese, divided
- ¼ cup salsa
- ¼ cup sour cream
- Cooking spray

1. Place the crisper tray on the air fry position. Select Air Fry, set the temperature to 400°F (204°C), and set the time to 10 minutes.

2. Put the sweet panatoes in a large bowl, then drizzle with vegetable oil and sprinkle with salt and black pepper. Toss to coat well.

3. Place the sweet panatoes in the crisper tray. Air fry for 10 minutes or until lightly browned. Shake the crisper tray halfway through.

4. Unfold the tortillas on a clean work surface. Divide the black beans, spinach, sweet panatoes, scrambled eggs, and cheese on top of the tortillas.

5. Fold the long side of the tortillas over the filling, then fold in the shorter side to wrap the filling to make the burritos.

6. Work in batches, wrap the burritos in the aluminum foil and put in the crisper tray.

7. Adjust the temperature to 350°F (177°C). Air fry for 20 minutes. Flip the burritos halfway through.

8. Remove the burritos from the grill and put back to the grill. Spritz with cooking spray and air fry for 5 more minutes or until lightly browned. Repeat with remaining burritos.

9. Remove the burritos from the grill and spread with sour

cream and salsa. Serve immediately.

Eggplant Hoagies

Prep time: 15 minutes | Cook time: 12 minutes | Makes 3 hoagies

- 6 peeled eggplant slices (about ½ inch thick and 3 inches in diameter)
- ¼ cup jarred pizza sauce
- 6 tablespoons grated

- Parmesan cheese
- 3 Italian sub rolls, split open lengthwise, warmed
- Cooking spray

1. Spritz the crisper tray with cooking spray.
2. Place the crisper tray on the air fry position. Select Air Fry, set the temperature to 350°F (177°C), and set the time to 10 minutes.
3. Arrange the eggplant slices in the crisper tray and spritz with cooking spray.
4. Air fry for 10 minutes or until lightly wilted and tender. Flip the slices halfway through.
5. Divide and spread the pizza sauce and cheese on top of the eggplant slice. Increase the temperature to 375°F (191°C). Air fry for 2 more minutes or until the cheese melts.
6. Assemble each sub roll with two slices of eggplant and serve immediately.

Montreal Steak and Seeds Burgers

Prep time: 15 minutes | Cook time: 10 minutes | Serves 4

- 1 teaspoon cumin seeds
- 1 teaspoon mustard seeds
- 1 teaspoon coriander seeds
- 1 teaspoon dried minced garlic
- 1 teaspoon dried red pepper flakes
- 1 teaspoon kosher salt
- 2 teaspoons ground black

- pepper
- 1 pound (454 g) 85% lean ground beef
- 2 tablespoons Worcestershire sauce
- 4 hamburger buns
- Mayonnaise, for serving
- Cooking spray

1. Spritz the crisper tray with cooking spray.
2. Place the crisper tray on the air fry position. Select Air Fry, set the temperature to 350°F (177°C), and set the time to 10 minutes.
3. Put the seeds, garlic, red pepper flakes, salt, and ground black pepper in a food processor. Pulse to coarsely ground the mixture.
4. Put the ground beef in a large bowl. Pour in the seed mixture and drizzle with Worcestershire sauce. Stir to mix well.
5. Divide the mixture into four parts and shape each part into a ball, then bash each ball into a patty.
6. Arrange the patties in the crisper tray. Air fry for 10 minutes or until the patties are well browned. Flip the patties with

tongs halfway through.

7. Assemble the buns with the patties, then drizzle the mayo over the patties to make the burgers. Serve immediately.

Turkey, Leek, and Pepper Hamburger

Prep time: 10 minutes | Cook time: 20 minutes | Serves 4

- 1 cup leftover turkey, cut into bite-sized chunks
- 1 leek, sliced
- 1 Serrano pepper, deveined and chopped
- 2 bell peppers, deveined and chopped
- 2 tablespoons Tabasco sauce
- ½ cup sour cream

- 1 heaping tablespoon fresh cilantro, chopped
- 1 teaspoon hot paprika
- ¾ teaspoon kosher salt
- ½ teaspoon ground black pepper
- 4 hamburger buns
- Cooking spray

1. Place the baking pan on the bake position. Select Bake, set the temperature to 385°F (196°C), and set the time to 20 minutes.
2. Spritz the baking pan with cooking spray.
3. Mix all the ingredients, except for the buns, in a large bowl. Toss to combine well.
4. Pour the mixture in the baking pan. Bake for 20 minutes, or until the turkey is well browned and the leek is tender.
5. Assemble the hamburger buns with the turkey mixture and serve immediately.

Turkey Sliders with Chive Mayo

Prep time: 10 minutes | Cook time: 15 minutes | Serves 6

- 12 burger buns
- Cooking spray

For the Turkey Sliders:

- ¾ pound (340 g) turkey, minced
- 1 tablespoon oyster sauce
- ¼ cup pickled jalapeno, chopped
- 2 tablespoons chopped scallions

- 1 tablespoon chopped fresh cilantro
- 1 to 2 cloves garlic, minced
- Sea salt and ground black pepper, to taste

For the Chive Mayo:

- 1 tablespoon chives
- 1 cup mayonnaise
- Zest of 1 lime
- 1 teaspoon salt

1. Place the crisper tray on the air fry position. Select Air Fry, set the temperature to 365°F (185°C), and set the time to 15 minutes.
2. Spritz the crisper tray with cooking spray.
3. Combine the ingredients for the turkey sliders in a large bowl. Stir to mix well. Shape the mixture into 6 balls, then bash the balls into patties.
4. Arrange the patties in the crisper tray and spritz with cook-

ing spray. Air fry for 15 minutes or until well browned. Flip the patties halfway through.

5. Meanwhile, combine the ingredients for the chive mayo in a small bowl. Stir to mix well.

6. Smear the patties with chive mayo, then assemble the patties between two buns to make the sliders. Serve immediately.

Gochujang Beef and Onion Tacos

Prep time: 1 hour 15 minutes | Cook time: 12 minutes | Serves 6

- 2 tablespoons gochujang
- 1 tablespoon soy sauce
- 2 tablespoons sesame seeds
- 2 teaspoons minced fresh ginger
- 2 cloves garlic, minced
- 2 tablespoons toasted sesame oil
- 2 teaspoons sugar
- ½ teaspoon kosher salt
- 1½ pounds (680 g) thinly sliced beef chuck
- 1 medium red onion, sliced
- 6 corn tortillas, warmed
- ¼ cup chopped fresh cilantro
- ½ cup kimchi
- ½ cup chopped green onions

1. Combine the gochujang, soy sauce, sesame seeds, ginger, garlic, sesame oil, sugar, and salt in a large bowl. Stir to mix well.

2. Dunk the beef chunk in the large bowl. Press to submerge, then wrap the bowl in plastic and refrigerate to marinate for at least 1 hour.

3. Remove the beef chunk from the marinade and transfer to the perforated pan. Add the onion to the pan.

4. Select Air Fry. Set temperature to 400°F (205°C) and set time to 12 minutes. Press Start to begin preheating.

5. Once preheated, place the pan into the oven. Stir the mixture halfway through the cooking time.

6. When cooked, the beef will be well browned.

7. Unfold the tortillas on a clean work surface, then divide the fried beef and onion on the tortillas. Spread the cilantro, kimchi, and green onions on top.

8. Serve immediately.

Curried Shrimp and Zucchini Potstickers

Prep time: 35 minutes | Cook time: 5 minutes | Serves 10

- ½ pound (227 g) peeled and deveined shrimp, finely chopped
- 1 medium zucchini, coarsely grated
- 1 tablespoon fish sauce
- 1 tablespoon green curry paste
- 2 scallions, thinly sliced
- ¼ cup basil, chopped
- 30 round dumpling wrappers
- Cooking spray

1. Combine the chopped shrimp, zucchini, fish sauce, curry paste, scallions, and basil in a large bowl. Stir to mix well.

2. Unfold the dumpling wrappers on a clean work surface, dab a little water around the edges of each wrapper, then scoop up 1 teaspoon of filling in the middle of each wrapper.

3. Make the potstickers: Fold the wrappers in half and press the edges to seal.

4. Spritz the perforated pan with cooking spray.

5. Transfer the potstickers to the pan and spritz with cooking spray.

6. Select Air Fry. Set temperature to 350°F (180°C) and set time to 5 minutes. Press Start to begin preheating.

7. Once preheated, place the pan into the oven. Flip the potstickers halfway through the cooking time.

8. When cooking is complete, the potstickers should be crunchy and lightly browned.

9. Serve immediately.

Cod Fish Tacos with Mango Salsa

Prep time: 15 minutes | Cook time: 17 minutes | Makes 6 tacos

- 1 egg
- 5 ounces (142 g) Mexican beer
- ¾ cup all-purpose flour
- ¾ cup cornstarch
- ¼ teaspoon chili powder
- ½ teaspoon ground cumin
- ½ pound (227 g) cod, cut into large pieces
- 6 corn tortillas
- Cooking spray

Salsa:
- 1 mango, peeled and diced
- ¼ red bell pepper, diced
- ½ small jalapeño, diced
- ¼ red onion, minced
- Juice of half a lime
- Pinch chopped fresh cilantro
- ¼ teaspoon salt
- ¼ teaspoon ground black pepper

1. Spritz the perforated pan with cooking spray.

2. Whisk the egg with beer in a bowl. Combine the flour, cornstarch, chili powder, and cumin in a separate bowl.

3. Dredge the cod in the egg mixture first, then in the flour mixture to coat well. Shake the excess off.

4. Arrange the cod in the perforated pan and spritz with cooking spray.

5. Select Air Fry. Set temperature to 380°F (193°C) and set time to 17 minutes. Press Start to begin preheating.

6. Once preheated, place the pan into the oven. Flip the cod halfway through the cooking time.

7. When cooked, the cod should be golden brown and crunchy.

8. Meanwhile, combine the ingredients for the salsa in a small bowl. Stir to mix well.

9. Unfold the tortillas on a clean work surface, then divide the fish on the tortillas and spread the salsa on top. Fold to serve.

Bacon and Egg Wraps with Salsa

Prep time: 15 minutes | Cook time: 10 minutes | Serves 3

- 3 corn tortillas
- 3 slices bacon, cut into strips
- 2 scrambled eggs
- 3 tablespoons salsa
- 1 cup grated Pepper Jack cheese
- 3 tablespoons cream cheese, divided
- Cooking spray

1. Spritz the perforated pan with cooking spray.

2. Unfold the tortillas on a clean work surface, divide the bacon and eggs in the middle of the tortillas, then spread with salsa and scatter with cheeses. Fold the tortillas over.

3. Arrange the tortillas in the pan.

4. Select Air Fry. Set temperature to 390°F (199°C) and set time to 10 minutes. Press Start to begin preheating.

5. Once the oven has preheated, place the pan into the oven. Flip the tortillas halfway through the cooking time.

6. When cooking is complete, the cheeses will be melted and the tortillas will be lightly browned.

7. Serve immediately.

Chicken Wraps with Ricotta Cheese

Prep time: 30 minutes | Cook time: 5 minutes | Serves 12

- 2 large-sized chicken breasts, cooked and shredded
- 2 spring onions, chopped
- 10 ounces (284 g) Ricotta cheese
- 1 tablespoon rice vinegar
- 1 tablespoon molasses
- 1 teaspoon grated fresh
- ginger
- ¼ cup soy sauce
- ⅓ teaspoon sea salt
- ¼ teaspoon ground black pepper, or more to taste
- 48 wonton wrappers
- Cooking spray

1. Spritz the perforated pan with cooking spray.

2. Combine all the ingredients, except for the wrappers in a large bowl. Toss to mix well.

3. Unfold the wrappers on a clean work surface, then divide and spoon the mixture in the middle of the wrappers.

4. Dab a little water on the edges of the wrappers, then fold the edge close to you over the filling. Tuck the edge under the filling and roll up to seal.

5. Arrange the wraps in the pan.

6. Select Air Fry. Set temperature to 375°F (190°C) and set time to 5 minutes. Press Start to begin preheating.

7. Once preheated, place the pan into the oven. Flip the wraps halfway through the cooking time.

8. When cooking is complete, the wraps should be lightly browned.

9. Serve immediately.

Sweet Potato and Spinach Burritos

Prep time: 15 minutes | Cook time: 30 minutes | Makes 6 burritos

- 2 sweet potatoes, peeled and cut into a small dice
- 1 tablespoon vegetable oil
- Kosher salt and ground black pepper, to taste
- 6 large flour tortillas
- 1 (16-ounce / 454-g) can refried black beans, divided
- 1½ cups baby spinach, divided
- 6 eggs, scrambled
- ¾ cup grated Cheddar cheese, divided
- ¼ cup salsa
- ¼ cup sour cream
- Cooking spray

1. Put the sweet potatoes in a large bowl, then drizzle with vegetable oil and sprinkle with salt and black pepper. Toss to coat well.

2. Place the potatoes in the perforated pan.

3. Select Air Fry. Set temperature to 400°F (205°C) and set time to 10 minutes. Press Start to begin preheating.

4. Once preheated, place the pan into the oven. Flip the potatoes halfway through the cooking time.

5. When done, the potatoes should be lightly browned. Remove the potatoes from the oven.

6. Unfold the tortillas on a clean work surface. Divide the black beans, spinach, air fried sweet potatoes, scrambled eggs, and cheese on top of the tortillas.

7. Fold the long side of the tortillas over the filling, then fold in the shorter side to wrap the filling to make the burritos.

8. Wrap the burritos in the aluminum foil and put in the pan.

9. Select Air Fry. Set temperature to 350°F (180°C) and set time to 20 minutes. Place the pan into the oven. Flip the burritos halfway through the cooking time.

10. Remove the burritos from the oven and spread with sour cream and salsa. Serve immediately.

Cabbage and Prawn Wraps

Prep time: 20 minutes | Cook time: 18 minutes | Serves 4

- 2 tablespoons olive oil
- 1 carrot, cut into strips
- 1-inch piece fresh ginger, grated
- 1 tablespoon minced garlic
- 2 tablespoons soy sauce
- ¼ cup chicken broth
- 1 tablespoon sugar
- 1 cup shredded Napa cabbage

- 1 tablespoon sesame oil
- 8 cooked prawns, minced
- 8 egg roll wrappers
- 1 egg, beaten
- Cooking spray

1. Spritz the perforated pan with cooking spray. Set aside.

2. Heat the olive oil in a nonstick skillet over medium heat until shimmering.

3. Add the carrot, ginger, and garlic and sauté for 2 minutes or until fragrant.

4. Pour in the soy sauce, broth, and sugar. Bring to a boil. Keep stirring.

5. Add the cabbage and simmer for 4 minutes or until the cabbage is tender.

6. Turn off the heat and mix in the sesame oil. Let sit for 15 minutes.

7. Use a strainer to remove the vegetables from the liquid, then combine with the minced prawns.

8. Unfold the egg roll wrappers on a clean work surface, then divide the prawn mixture in the center of wrappers.

9. Dab the edges of a wrapper with the beaten egg, then fold a corner over the filling and tuck the corner under the filling. Fold the left and right corner into the center. Roll the wrapper up and press to seal. Repeat with remaining wrappers.

10. Arrange the wrappers in the pan and spritz with cooking spray.

11. Select Air Fry. Set temperature to 370°F (188°C) and set time to 12 minutes. Press Start to begin preheating.

12. Once the oven has preheated, place the pan into the oven. Flip the wrappers halfway through the cooking time.

13. When cooking is complete, the wrappers should be golden.

14. Serve immediately.

Ricotta Spinach and Basil Pockets

Prep time: 20 minutes | Cook time: 10 minutes | Makes 8 pockets

- 2 large eggs, divided
- 1 tablespoon water
- 1 cup baby spinach, roughly chopped
- ¼ cup sun-dried tomatoes, finely chopped
- 1 cup ricotta cheese
- 1 cup basil, chopped
- ¼ teaspoon red pepper flakes
- ¼ teaspoon kosher salt
- 2 refrigerated rolled pie crusts
- 2 tablespoons sesame seeds

1. Spritz the perforated pan with cooking spray.

2. Whisk an egg with water in a small bowl.

3. Combine the spinach, tomatoes, the other egg, ricotta

cheese, basil, red pepper flakes, and salt in a large bowl. Whisk to mix well.

4. Unfold the pie crusts on a clean work surface and slice each crust into 4 wedges. Scoop up 3 tablespoons of the spinach mixture on each crust and leave ½ inch space from edges.

5. Fold the crust wedges in half to wrap the filling and press the edges with a fork to seal.

6. Arrange the wraps in the pan and spritz with cooking spray. Sprinkle with sesame seeds.

7. Select Air Fry. Set temperature to 380°F (193°C) and set time to 10 minutes. Press Start to begin preheating.

8. Once the oven has preheated, place the pan into the oven. Flip the wraps halfway through the cooking time.

9. When cooked, the wraps will be crispy and golden.

10. Serve immediately.

Carrot and Mushroom Spring Rolls

Prep time: 10 minutes | Cook time: 18 minutes | Serves 4

- 4 spring roll wrappers
- ½ cup cooked vermicelli noodles
- 1 teaspoon sesame oil
- 1 tablespoon freshly minced ginger
- 1 tablespoon soy sauce
- 1 clove garlic, minced
- ½ red bell pepper, deseeded and chopped
- ½ cup chopped carrot
- ½ cup chopped mushrooms
- ¼ cup chopped scallions
- Cooking spray

1. Spritz the perforated pan with cooking spray and set aside.

2. Heat the sesame oil in a saucepan on medium heat. Sauté the ginger and garlic in the sesame oil for 1 minute, or until fragrant. Add soy sauce, red bell pepper, carrot, mushrooms and scallions. Sauté for 5 minutes or until the vegetables become tender. Mix in vermicelli noodles. Turn off the heat and remove them from the saucepan. Allow to cool for 10 minutes.

3. Lay out one spring roll wrapper with a corner pointed toward you. Scoop the noodle mixture on spring roll wrapper and fold corner up over the mixture. Fold left and right corners toward the center and continue to roll to make firmly sealed rolls.

4. Arrange the spring rolls in the pan and spritz with cooking spray.

5. Select Air Fry. Set temperature to 340°F (171°C) and set time to 12 minutes. Press Start to begin preheating.

6. Once the oven has preheated, place the pan into the oven. Flip the spring rolls halfway through the cooking time.

7. When done, the spring rolls will be golden brown and crispy.

8. Serve warm.

Avocado and Tomato Wraps

Prep time: 10 minutes | Cook time: 5 minutes | Serves 5

- 10 egg roll wrappers
- 3 avocados, peeled and pitted
- 1 tomato, diced
- Salt and ground black pepper, to taste
- Cooking spray

1. Spritz the perforated pan with cooking spray.

2. Put the tomato and avocados in a food processor. Sprinkle with salt and ground black pepper. Pulse to mix and coarsely mash until smooth.

3. Unfold the wrappers on a clean work surface, then divide the mixture in the center of each wrapper. Roll the wrapper up and press to seal.

4. Transfer the rolls to the pan and spritz with cooking spray.

5. Select Air Fry. Set temperature to 350°F (180°C) and set time to 5 minutes. Press Start to begin preheating.

6. Once the oven has preheated, place the pan into the oven. Flip the rolls halfway through the cooking time.

7. When cooked, the rolls should be golden brown.

8. Serve immediately.

Chicken and Cabbage Wraps

Prep time: 10 minutes | Cook time: 23 to 24 minutes | Serves 4

- 1 pound (454 g) ground chicken
- 2 teaspoons olive oil
- 2 garlic cloves, minced
- 1 teaspoon grated fresh ginger
- 2 cups white cabbage, shredded
- 1 onion, chopped
- ¼ cup soy sauce
- 8 egg roll wrappers
- 1 egg, beaten
- Cooking spray

1. Spritz the perforated pan with cooking spray.

2. Heat olive oil in a saucepan over medium heat. Sauté the garlic and ginger in the olive oil for 1 minute, or until fragrant. Add the ground chicken to the saucepan. Sauté for 5 minutes, or until the chicken is cooked through. Add the cabbage, onion and soy sauce and sauté for 5 to 6 minutes, or until the vegetables become soft. Remove the saucepan from the heat.

3. Unfold the egg roll wrappers on a clean work surface. Divide the chicken mixture among the wrappers and brush the edges of the wrappers with the beaten egg. Tightly roll up the egg rolls, enclosing the filling. Arrange the rolls in the pan.

4. Select Air Fry. Set temperature to 370°F (188°C) and set time to 12 minutes. Press Start to begin preheating.

5. Once the oven has preheated, place the pan into the oven. Flip the rolls halfway through the cooking time.

6. When cooked, the rolls will be crispy and golden brown.

7. Transfer to a platter and let cool for 5 minutes before serving.

Cajun Beef and Bell Pepper Fajitas

Prep time: 15 minutes | Cook time: 10 minutes | Serves 4

- 1 pound (454 g) beef sirloin steak, cut into strips
- 2 shallots, sliced
- 1 orange bell pepper, sliced
- 1 red bell pepper, sliced
- 2 garlic cloves, minced
- 2 tablespoons Cajun seasoning
- 1 tablespoon paprika
- Salt and ground black pepper, to taste
- 4 corn tortillas
- ½ cup shredded Cheddar cheese
- Cooking spray

1. Spritz the perforated pan with cooking spray.

2. Combine all the ingredients, except for the tortillas and cheese, in a large bowl. Toss to coat well.

3. Pour the beef and vegetables in the pan and spritz with cooking spray.

4. Select Air Fry. Set temperature to 360°F (182°C) and set time to 10 minutes. Press Start to begin preheating.

5. Once preheated, place the pan into the oven. Stir the beef and vegetables halfway through the cooking time.

6. When cooking is complete, the meat will be browned and the vegetables will be soft and lightly wilted.

7. Unfold the tortillas on a clean work surface and spread the cooked beef and vegetables on top. Scatter with cheese and fold to serve.

Potato Taquitos with Mexican Cheese

Prep time: 5 minutes | Cook time: 6 minutes | Makes 12 taquitos

- 2 cups mashed potatoes
- ½ cup shredded Mexican cheese
- 12 corn tortillas
- Cooking spray

1. Line a baking pan with parchment paper.

2. In a bowl, combine the potatoes and cheese until well mixed. Microwave the tortillas on high heat for 30 seconds, or until softened. Add some water to another bowl and set alongside.

3. On a clean work surface, lay the tortillas. Scoop 3 tablespoons of the potato mixture in the center of each tortilla. Roll up tightly and secure with toothpicks if necessary.

4. Arrange the filled tortillas, seam side down, in the prepared baking pan. Spritz the tortillas with cooking spray.

5. Select Air Fry. Set temperature to 400°F (205°C) and set

time to 6 minutes. Press Start to begin preheating.

6. Once preheated, place the pan into the oven. Flip the tortillas halfway through the cooking time.

7. When cooked, the tortillas should be crispy and golden brown.

8. Serve hot.

Chickpea and Mushroom Wraps

Prep time: 15 minutes | Cook time: 9 minutes | Serves 4

- 8 ounces (227 g) green beans
- 2 portobello mushroom caps, sliced
- 1 large red pepper, sliced
- 2 tablespoons olive oil, divided
- ¼ teaspoon salt
- 1 (15-ounce / 425-g) can chickpeas, drained
- 3 tablespoons lemon juice
- ¼ teaspoon ground black pepper
- 4 (6-inch) whole-grain wraps
- 4 ounces (113 g) fresh herb or garlic goat cheese, crumbled
- 1 lemon, cut into wedges

1. Add the green beans, mushrooms, red pepper to a large bowl. Drizzle with 1 tablespoon olive oil and season with salt. Toss until well coated.

2. Transfer the vegetable mixture to a baking pan.

3. Select Air Fry. Set temperature to 400°F (205°C) and set time to 9 minutes. Press Start to begin preheating.

4. Once preheated, slide the pan into the oven. Stir the vegetable mixture three times during cooking.

5. When cooked, the vegetables should be tender.

6. Meanwhile, mash the chickpeas with lemon juice, pepper and the remaining 1 tablespoon oil until well blended

7. Unfold the wraps on a clean work surface. Spoon the chickpea mash on the wraps and spread all over.

8. Divide the cooked veggies among wraps. Sprinkle 1 ounce crumbled goat cheese on top of each wrap. Fold to wrap. Squeeze the lemon wedges on top and serve.

Mozzarella Chicken Taquitos

Prep time: 15 minutes | Cook time: 12 minutes | Serves 4

- 1 cup cooked chicken, shredded
- ¼ cup Greek yogurt
- ¼ cup salsa
- 1 cup shredded Mozzarella
- cheese
- Salt and ground black pepper, to taste
- 4 flour tortillas
- Cooking spray

1. Spritz the perforated pan with cooking spray.

2. Combine all the ingredients, except for the tortillas, in a large bowl. Stir to mix well.

3. Make the taquitos: Unfold the tortillas on a clean work surface, then scoop up 2 tablespoons of the chicken mixture in the middle of each tortilla. Roll the tortillas up to wrap the filling.

4. Arrange the taquitos in the pan and spritz with cooking spray.

5. Select Nuwave Air Fryer Oven. Set temperature to 380°F (193°C) and set time to 12 minutes. Press Start to begin preheating.

6. Once preheated, place the pan into the oven. Flip the taquitos halfway through the cooking time.

7. When cooked, the taquitos should be golden brown and the cheese should be melted.

8. Serve immediately.

Curried Pork Sliders

Prep time: 10 minutes | Cook time: 14 minutes | Makes 6 sliders

- 1 pound (454 g) ground pork
- 1 tablespoon Thai curry paste
- 1½ tablespoons fish sauce
- ¼ cup thinly sliced scallions, white and green parts
- 2 tablespoons minced
- peeled fresh ginger
- 1 tablespoon light brown sugar
- 1 teaspoon ground black pepper
- 6 slider buns, split open lengthwise, warmed
- Cooking spray

1. Spritz the perforated pan with cooking spray.

2. Combine all the ingredients, except for the buns in a large bowl. Stir to mix well.

3. Divide and shape the mixture into six balls, then bash the balls into six 3-inch-diameter patties.

4. Arrange the patties in the pan and spritz with cooking spray.

5. Select Nuwave Air Fryer Oven. Set temperature to 375°F (190°C) and set time to 14 minutes. Press Start to begin preheating.

6. Once the oven has preheated, place the pan into the oven. Flip the patties halfway through the cooking time.

7. When cooked, the patties should be well browned.

8. Assemble the buns with patties to make the sliders and serve immediately.

Pork Momos with Carrot

Prep time: 20 minutes | Cook time: 20 minutes | Serves 4

- 2 tablespoons olive oil
- 1 pound (454 g) ground pork
- 1 shredded carrot
- 1 onion, chopped
- 1 teaspoon soy sauce

- 16 wonton wrappers
- Salt and ground black
- pepper, to taste
- Cooking spray

1. Heat the olive oil in a nonstick skillet over medium heat until shimmering.

2. Add the ground pork, carrot, onion, soy sauce, salt, and ground black pepper and sauté for 10 minutes or until the pork is well browned and carrots are tender.

3. Unfold the wrappers on a clean work surface, then divide the cooked pork and vegetables on the wrappers. Fold the edges around the filling to form momos. Nip the top to seal the momos.

4. Arrange the momos in the perforated pan and spritz with cooking spray.

5. Select Nuwave Air Fryer Oven. Set temperature to 320°F (160°C) and set time to 10 minutes. Press Start to begin preheating.

6. Once the oven has preheated, place the pan into the oven.

7. When cooking is complete, the wrappers will be lightly browned.

8. Serve immediately.

Crispy Cream Cheese Wontons

Prep time: 5 minutes | Cook time: 6 minutes | Serves 4

- 2 ounces (57 g) cream cheese, softened
- 1 tablespoon sugar
- 16 square wonton wrappers
- Cooking spray

1. Spritz the perforated pan with cooking spray.

2. In a mixing bowl, stir together the cream cheese and sugar until well mixed. Prepare a small bowl of water alongside.

3. On a clean work surface, lay the wonton wrappers. Scoop ¼ teaspoon of cream cheese in the center of each wonton wrapper. Dab the water over the wrapper edges. Fold each wonton wrapper diagonally in half over the filling to form a triangle.

4. Arrange the wontons in the pan. Spritz the wontons with cooking spray.

5. Select Nuwave Air Fryer Oven. Set temperature to 350°F (180°C) and set time to 6 minutes. Press Start to begin preheating.

6. Once preheated, place the pan into the oven. Flip the wontons halfway through the cooking time.

7. When cooking is complete, the wontons will be golden brown and crispy.

8. Divide the wontons among four plates. Let rest for 5 minutes before serving.

Wraps and Sandwiches

Chapter 5 Vegan and Vegetarian

Cayenne Green Beans

Prep time: 5 minutes | Cook time: 15 minutes | Serves 4

- ½ cup flour
- 2 eggs
- 1 cup panko bread crumbs
- ½ cup grated Parmesan cheese
- 1 teaspoon cayenne pepper
- Salt and black pepper, to taste
- 1½ pounds (680 g) green beans

1. In a bowl, place the flour. In a separate bowl, lightly beat the eggs. In a separate shallow bowl, thoroughly combine the bread crumbs, cheese, cayenne pepper, salt, and pepper.

2. Dip the green beans in the flour, then in the beaten eggs, finally in the bread crumb mixture to coat well. Transfer the green beans to the perforated pan.

3. Select Air Fry. Set temperature to 400°F (205°C) and set time to 15 minutes. Press Start to begin preheating.

4. Once preheated, place the pan into the oven. Stir the green beans halfway through the cooking time.

5. When cooking is complete, remove from the oven to a bowl and serve.

Honey Baby Carrots with Dill

Prep time: 5 minutes | Cook time: 12 minutes | Serves 4

- 1 pound (454 g) baby carrots
- 2 tablespoons olive oil
- 1 tablespoon honey
- 1 teaspoon dried dill
- Salt and black pepper, to taste

1. Place the carrots in a large bowl. Add the olive oil, honey, dill, salt, and pepper and toss to coat well.

2. Transfer the carrots to the perforated pan.

3. Select Roast. Set temperature to 350°F (180°C) and set time to 12 minutes. Press Start to begin preheating.

4. Once preheated, place the pan into the oven. Stir the carrots once during cooking.

5. When cooking is complete, the carrots should be crisp-tender. Remove from the oven and serve warm.

Garlic Tofu with Basil

Prep time: 5 minutes | Cook time: 10 minutes | Serves 2

- 1 tablespoon soy sauce
- 1 tablespoon water
- ⅓ teaspoon garlic powder
- ⅓ teaspoon onion powder
- ⅓ teaspoon dried oregano
- ⅓ teaspoon dried basil
- Black pepper, to taste
- 6 ounces (170 g) extra firm tofu, pressed and cubed

1. In a large mixing bowl, whisk together the soy sauce, water, garlic powder, onion powder, oregano, basil, and black pepper. Add the tofu cubes, stirring to coat, and let them marinate for 10 minutes.

2. Arrange the tofu in the perforated pan.

3. Select Bake. Set temperature to 390ºF (199ºC) and set time to 10 minutes. Press Start to begin preheating.

4. Once preheated, place the pan into the oven. Flip the tofu halfway through the cooking time.

5. When cooking is complete, the tofu should be crisp.

6. Remove from the oven to a plate and serve.

Zucchini Quesadilla with Gouda Cheese

Prep time: 5 minutes | Cook time: 10 minutes | Serves 1

- 1 teaspoon olive oil
- 2 flour tortillas
- ¼ zucchini, sliced
- ¼ yellow bell pepper, sliced
- ¼ cup shredded Gouda cheese
- 1 tablespoon chopped cilantro
- ½ green onion, sliced

1. Coat the perforated pan with 1 teaspoon of olive oil.

2. Arrange a flour tortilla in the perforated pan and scatter the top with zucchini, bell pepper, Gouda cheese, cilantro, and green onion. Place the other flour tortilla on top.

3. Select Air Fry. Set temperature to 390ºF (199ºC) and set time to 10 minutes. Press Start to begin preheating.

4. Once preheated, place the pan into the oven.

5. When cooking is complete, the tortillas should be lightly browned and the vegetables should be tender. Remove from the oven and cool for 5 minutes before slicing into wedges.

Curried Cauliflower with Cashews

Prep time: 5 minutes | Cook time: 12 minutes | Serves 2

- 4 cups cauliflower florets (about half a large head)
- 1 tablespoon olive oil
- 1 teaspoon curry powder
- Salt, to taste
- ½ cup toasted, chopped cashews, for garnish

Yogurt Sauce:
- ¼ cup plain yogurt

- 2 tablespoons sour cream
- 1 teaspoon honey
- 1 teaspoon lemon juice
- Pinch cayenne pepper
- Salt, to taste
- 1 tablespoon chopped fresh cilantro, plus leaves for garnish

1. In a large mixing bowl, toss the cauliflower florets with the olive oil, curry powder, and salt.

2. Place the cauliflower florets in the perforated pan.

3. Select Air Fry. Set temperature to 400ºF (205ºC) and set time to 12 minutes. Press Start to begin preheating.

4. Once preheated, place the pan into the oven. Stir the cauliflower florets twice during cooking.

5. When cooking is complete, the cauliflower should be golden brown.

6. Meanwhile, mix all the ingredients for the yogurt sauce in a small bowl and whisk to combine.

7. Remove the cauliflower from the oven and drizzle with the yogurt sauce. Scatter the toasted cashews and cilantro on top and serve immediately.

Fried Root Veggies with Thyme

Prep time: 10 minutes | Cook time: 22 minutes | Serves 4

- 2 carrots, sliced
- 2 potatoes, cut into chunks
- 1 rutabaga, cut into chunks
- 1 turnip, cut into chunks
- 1 beet, cut into chunks
- 8 shallots, halved
- 2 tablespoons olive oil
- Salt and black pepper, to taste
- 2 tablespoons tomato pesto
- 2 tablespoons water
- 2 tablespoons chopped fresh thyme

1. Toss the carrots, potatoes, rutabaga, turnip, beet, shallots, olive oil, salt, and pepper in a large mixing bowl until the root vegetables are evenly coated.

2. Place the root vegetables in the perforated pan.

3. Select Air Fry. Set temperature to 400ºF (205ºC) and set time to 22 minutes. Press Start to begin preheating.

4. Once preheated, place the pan into the oven. Stir the vegetables twice during cooking.

5. When cooking is complete, the vegetables should be tender.

6. Meanwhile, in a small bowl, whisk together the tomato pesto and water until smooth.

7. When ready, remove the root vegetables from the oven to a platter. Drizzle with the tomato pesto mixture and sprinkle with the thyme. Serve immediately.

Red Chili Okra

Prep time: 5 minutes | Cook time: 10 minutes | Serves 4

- 3 tablespoons sour cream
- 2 tablespoons flour
- 2 tablespoons semolina
- ½ teaspoon red chili powder
- Salt and black pepper, to taste
- 1 pound (454 g) okra, halved
- Cooking spray

1. Spray the perforated pan with cooking spray. Set aside.

2. In a shallow bowl, place the sour cream. In another shallow bowl, thoroughly combine the flour, semolina, red chili powder, salt, and pepper.

3. Dredge the okra in the sour cream, then roll in the flour mixture until evenly coated. Transfer the okra to the perforated pan.

4. Select Air Fry. Set temperature to 400°F (205°C) and set time to 10 minutes. Press Start to begin preheating.

5. Once preheated, place the pan into the oven. Flip the okra halfway through the cooking time.

6. When cooking is complete, the okra should be golden brown and crispy. Remove the pan from the oven. Cool for 5 minutes before serving.

Veggie and Oat Meatballs

Prep time: 15 minutes | Cook time: 18 minutes | Serves 3

- ½ cup grated carrots
- ½ cup sweet onions
- 2 tablespoons olive oil
- 1 cup rolled oats
- ½ cup roasted cashews
- 2 cups cooked chickpeas
- Juice of 1 lemon
- 2 tablespoons soy sauce
- 1 tablespoon flax meal
- 1 teaspoon garlic powder
- 1 teaspoon cumin
- ½ teaspoon turmeric

1. Mix the carrots, onions, and olive oil in a baking dish and stir to combine.

2. Select Roast. Set temperature to 350°F (180°C) and set time to 6 minutes. Press Start to begin preheating.

3. Once preheated, place the baking dish into the oven. Stir the vegetables halfway through.

4. When cooking is complete, the vegetables should be tender.

5. Meanwhile, put the oats and cashews in a food processor or blender and pulse until coarsely ground. Transfer the mixture to a large bowl. Add the chickpeas, lemon juice, and soy sauce to the food processor and pulse until smooth. Transfer the chickpea mixture to the bowl of oat and cashew mixture.

6. Remove the carrots and onions from the oven to the bowl of chickpea mixture. Add the flax meal, garlic powder, cumin, and turmeric and stir to incorporate.

7. Scoop tablespoon-sized portions of the veggie mixture and roll them into balls with your hands. Transfer the balls to the perforated pan.

8. Increase the temperature to 370°F (188°C) and set time to 12 minutes on Bake. Place the pan into the oven. Flip the balls halfway through the cooking time.

9. When cooking is complete, the balls should be golden brown.

10. Serve warm.

Garlic Bell Peppers with Marjoram

Prep time: 10 minutes | Cook time: 22 minutes | Serves 4

- 1 green bell pepper, sliced into 1-inch strips
- 1 red bell pepper, sliced into 1-inch strips
- 1 orange bell pepper, sliced into 1-inch strips
- 1 yellow bell pepper, sliced into 1-inch strips
- 2 tablespoons olive oil, divided
- ½ teaspoon dried marjoram
- Pinch salt
- Freshly ground black pepper, to taste
- 1 head garlic

1. Toss the bell peppers with 1 tablespoon of olive oil in a large bowl until well coated. Season with the marjoram, salt, and pepper. Toss again and set aside.

2. Cut off the top of a head of garlic. Place the garlic cloves on a large square of aluminum foil. Drizzle the top with the remaining 1 tablespoon of olive oil and wrap the garlic cloves in foil.

3. Transfer the garlic to the perforated pan.

4. Select Roast. Set temperature to 330°F (166°C) and set time to 15 minutes. Press Start to begin preheating.

5. Once preheated, place the pan into the oven.

6. After 15 minutes, remove the perforated pan from the oven and add the bell peppers. Return to the oven and set time to 7 minutes.

7. When cooking is complete or until the garlic is soft and the bell peppers are tender.

8. Transfer the cooked bell peppers to a plate. Remove the garlic and unwrap the foil. Let the garlic rest for a few minutes. Once cooled, squeeze the roasted garlic cloves out of their skins and add them to the plate of bell peppers. Stir well and serve immediately.

Carrot, Tofu and Cauliflower Rice

Prep time: 10 minutes | Cook time: 22 minutes | Serves 4

- ½ block tofu, crumbled
- 1 cup diced carrot
- ½ cup diced onions
- 2 tablespoons soy sauce
- 1 teaspoon turmeric

Cauliflower:

- 3 cups cauliflower rice
- ½ cup chopped broccoli
- ½ cup frozen peas
- 2 tablespoons soy sauce
- 1 tablespoon minced ginger
- 2 garlic cloves, minced
- 1 tablespoon rice vinegar
- 1½ teaspoons toasted sesame oil

1. Mix the tofu, carrot, onions, soy sauce, and turmeric in a baking dish and stir until well incorporated.

2. Select Roast. Set temperature to 370°F (188°C) and set time to 10 minutes. Press Start to begin preheating.

3. Once preheated, place the baking dish into the oven. Flip the tofu and carrot halfway through the cooking time.

4. When cooking is complete, the tofu should be crisp.

5. Meanwhile, in a large bowl, combine all the ingredients for

the cauliflower and toss well.

6. Remove the dish from the oven and add the cauliflower mixture to the tofu and stir to combine.

7. Return the baking dish to the oven and set time to 12 minutes on Roast. Place the baking dish into the oven

8. When cooking is complete, the vegetables should be tender.

9. Cool for 5 minutes before serving.

Halloumi Zucchinis and Eggplant

Prep time: 5 minutes | Cook time: 14 minutes | Serves 2

- 2 zucchinis, cut into even chunks
- 1 large eggplant, peeled, cut into chunks
- 1 large carrot, cut into chunks
- 6 ounces (170 g) halloumi
- cheese, cubed
- 2 teaspoons olive oil
- Salt and black pepper, to taste
- 1 teaspoon dried mixed herbs

1. Combine the zucchinis, eggplant, carrot, cheese, olive oil, salt, and pepper in a large bowl and toss to coat well.

2. Spread the mixture evenly in the perforated pan.

3. Select Air Fry. Set temperature to 340°F (171°C) and set time to 14 minutes. Press Start to begin preheating.

4. Once preheated, place the pan into the oven. Stir the mixture once during cooking.

5. When cooking is complete, they should be crispy and golden. Remove from the oven and serve topped with mixed herbs.

Breaded Zucchini Chips with Parmesan

Prep time: 5 minutes | Cook time: 14 minutes | Serves 4

- 2 egg whites
- Salt and black pepper, to taste
- ½ cup seasoned bread crumbs
- 2 tablespoons grated
- Parmesan cheese
- ¼ teaspoon garlic powder
- 2 medium zucchini, sliced
- Cooking spray

1. Spritz the perforated pan with cooking spray.

2. In a bowl, beat the egg whites with salt and pepper. In a separate bowl, thoroughly combine the bread crumbs, Parmesan cheese, and garlic powder.

3. Dredge the zucchini slices in the egg white, then coat in the bread crumb mixture.

4. Arrange the zucchini slices in the perforated pan.

5. Select Air Fry. Set temperature to 400°F (205°C) and set time to 14 minutes. Press Start to begin preheating.

6. Once preheated, place the pan into the oven. Flip the zucchini halfway through.

7. When cooking is complete, the zucchini should be tender.

8. Remove from the oven to a plate and serve.

Roasted Veggies with Honey-Garlic Glaze

Prep time: 15 minutes | Cook time: 20 minutes | Makes 3 cups

Glaze:

- 2 tablespoons raw honey
- 2 teaspoons minced garlic
- ¼ teaspoon dried marjoram
- ¼ teaspoon dried basil
- ¼ teaspoon dried oregano
- ⅛ teaspoon dried sage
- ⅛ teaspoon dried rosemary
- ⅛ teaspoon dried thyme
- ½ teaspoon salt
- ¼ teaspoon ground black pepper

Veggies:

- 3 to 4 medium red potatoes, cut into 1- to 2-inch pieces
- 1 small zucchini, cut into 1- to 2-inch pieces
- 1 small carrot, sliced into ¼-inch rounds
- 1 (10.5-ounce / 298-g) package cherry tomatoes, halved
- 1 cup sliced mushrooms
- 3 tablespoons olive oil

1. Combine the honey, garlic, marjoram, basil, oregano, sage, rosemary, thyme, salt, and pepper in a small bowl and stir to mix well. Set aside.

2. Place the red potatoes, zucchini, carrot, cherry tomatoes, and mushroom in a large bowl. Drizzle with the olive oil and toss to coat.

3. Pour the veggies into the perforated pan.

4. Select Roast. Set temperature to 380°F (193°C) and set time to 15 minutes. Press Start to begin preheating.

5. Once preheated, place the pan into the oven. Stir the veggies halfway through.

6. When cooking is complete, the vegetables should be tender.

7. When ready, transfer the roasted veggies to the large bowl. Pour the honey mixture over the veggies, tossing to coat.

8. Spread out the veggies in a baking pan and place in the oven.

9. Increase the temperature to 390°F (199°C) and set time to 5 minutes on Roast. Place the pan into the oven.

10. When cooking is complete, the veggies should be tender and glazed. Serve warm.

Garlic Ratatouille

Prep time: 15 minutes | Cook time: 16 minutes | Serves 2

- 2 Roma tomatoes, thinly sliced
- 1 zucchini, thinly sliced
- 2 yellow bell peppers,

sliced

- 2 garlic cloves, minced
- 2 tablespoons olive oil
- 2 tablespoons herbes de

Provence

- 1 tablespoon vinegar
- Salt and black pepper, to taste

1. Place the tomatoes, zucchini, bell peppers, garlic, olive oil, herbes de Provence, and vinegar in a large bowl and toss until the vegetables are evenly coated. Sprinkle with salt and pepper and toss again. Pour the vegetable mixture into a baking dish.

2. Select Roast. Set temperature to 390°F (199°C) and set time to 16 minutes. Press Start to begin preheating.

3. Once preheated, place the baking dish into the oven. Stir the vegetables halfway through.

4. When cooking is complete, the vegetables should be tender.

5. Let the vegetable mixture stand for 5 minutes in the oven before removing and serving.

Cauliflower with Teriyaki Sauce

Prep time: 5 minutes | Cook time: 14 minutes | Serves 4

- ½ cup soy sauce
- ⅓ cup water
- 1 tablespoon brown sugar
- 1 teaspoon sesame oil
- 1 teaspoon cornstarch

- 2 cloves garlic, chopped
- ½ teaspoon chili powder
- 1 big cauliflower head, cut into florets

1. Make the teriyaki sauce: In a small bowl, whisk together the soy sauce, water, brown sugar, sesame oil, cornstarch, garlic, and chili powder until well combined.

2. Place the cauliflower florets in a large bowl and drizzle the top with the prepared teriyaki sauce and toss to coat well.

3. Put the cauliflower florets in the perforated pan.

4. Select Air Fry. Set temperature to 340°F (171°C) and set time to 14 minutes. Press Start to begin preheating.

5. Once preheated, place the pan into the oven. Stir the cauliflower halfway through.

6. When cooking is complete, the cauliflower should be crisp-tender.

7. Let the cauliflower cool for 5 minutes before serving.

Onion-Stuffed Mushrooms

Prep time: 5 minutes | Cook time: 12 minutes | Serves 2

- 18 medium-sized white mushrooms
- 1 small onion, peeled and chopped
- 4 garlic cloves, peeled and minced

- 2 tablespoons olive oil
- 2 teaspoons cumin powder
- A pinch ground allspice
- Fine sea salt and freshly ground black pepper, to

taste

1. On a clean work surface, remove the mushroom stems. Using a spoon, scoop out the mushroom gills and discard.

2. Thoroughly combine the onion, garlic, olive oil, cumin powder, allspice, salt, and pepper in a mixing bowl. Stuff the mushrooms evenly with the mixture.

3. Place the stuffed mushrooms in the perforated pan.

4. Select Roast. Set temperature to 345°F (174°C) and set time to 12 minutes. Press Start to begin preheating.

5. Once preheated, place the pan into the oven.

6. When cooking is complete, the mushroom should be browned.

7. Cool for 5 minutes before serving.

Garlic Turnip and Zucchini

Prep time: 5 minutes | Cook time: 18 minutes | Serves 4

- 3 turnips, sliced
- 1 large zucchini, sliced
- 1 large red onion, cut into rings

- 2 cloves garlic, crushed
- 1 tablespoon olive oil
- Salt and black pepper, to taste

1. Put the turnips, zucchini, red onion, and garlic in a baking pan. Drizzle the olive oil over the top and sprinkle with the salt and pepper.

2. Select Bake. Set temperature to 330°F (166°C) and set time to 18 minutes. Press Start to begin preheating.

3. Once preheated, place the pan into the oven.

4. When cooking is complete, the vegetables should be tender. Remove from the oven and serve on a plate.

Balsamic-Glazed Beets

Prep time: 5 minutes | Cook time: 10 minutes | Serves 2

Beet:

- 2 beets, cubed
- 2 tablespoons olive oil
- 2 springs rosemary, chopped

- Salt and black pepper, to taste

Balsamic Glaze:

- ⅓ cup balsamic vinegar
- 1 tablespoon honey

1. Combine the beets, olive oil, rosemary, salt, and pepper in a mixing bowl and toss until the beets are completely coated.

2. Place the beets in the perforated pan.

3. Select Air Fry. Set temperature to 400°F (205°C) and set time to 10 minutes. Press Start to begin preheating.

4. Once preheated, place the pan into the oven. Stir the vegetables halfway through.

5. When cooking is complete, the beets should be crisp and browned at the edges.

6. Meanwhile, make the balsamic glaze: Place the balsamic vinegar and honey in a small saucepan and bring to a boil over medium heat. When the sauce boils, reduce the heat to medium-low heat and simmer until the liquid is reduced by half.

7. When ready, remove the beets from the oven to a platter. Pour the balsamic glaze over the top and serve immediately.

Mozzarella Walnut Stuffed Mushrooms

Prep time: 5 minutes | Cook time: 10 minutes | Serves 4

- 4 large portobello mushrooms
- 1 tablespoon canola oil
- ½ cup shredded Mozzarella cheese
- ⅓ cup minced walnuts
- 2 tablespoons chopped fresh parsley
- Cooking spray

1. Spritz the perforated pan with cooking spray.

2. On a clean work surface, remove the mushroom stems. Scoop out the gills with a spoon and discard. Coat the mushrooms with canola oil. Top each mushroom evenly with the shredded Mozzarella cheese, followed by the minced walnuts.

3. Arrange the mushrooms in the perforated pan.

4. Select Roast. Set temperature to 350°F (180°C) and set time to 10 minutes. Press Start to begin preheating.

5. Once preheated, place the pan into the oven.

6. When cooking is complete, the mushroom should be golden brown.

7. Transfer the mushrooms to a plate and sprinkle the parsley on top for garnish before serving.

Tomato-Stuffed Portobello Mushrooms

Prep time: 5 minutes | Cook time: 8 minutes | Serves 4

- 4 portobello mushrooms, stem removed
- 1 tablespoon olive oil
- 1 tomato, diced
- ½ green bell pepper, diced
- ½ small red onion, diced
- ½ teaspoon garlic powder
- Salt and black pepper, to taste
- ½ cup grated Mozzarella cheese

1. Using a spoon to scoop out the gills of the mushrooms and discard them. Brush the mushrooms with the olive oil.

2. In a mixing bowl, stir together the remaining ingredients except the Mozzarella cheese. Using a spoon to stuff each mushroom with the filling and scatter the Mozzarella cheese on top.

3. Arrange the mushrooms in the perforated pan.

4. Select Roast. Set temperature to 330°F (166°C) and set time to 8 minutes. Press Start to begin preheating.

5. Once preheated, place the pan into the oven.

6. When cooking is complete, the cheese should be melted.

7. Serve warm.

Roasted Veggie Salad with Lemon

Prep time: 5 minutes | Cook time: 20 minutes | Serves 2

- 1 potato, chopped
- 1 carrot, sliced diagonally
- 1 cup cherry tomatoes
- ½ small beetroot, sliced
- ¼ onion, sliced
- ½ teaspoon turmeric
- ½ teaspoon cumin
- ¼ teaspoon sea salt
- 2 tablespoons olive oil, divided
- A handful of arugula
- A handful of baby spinach
- Juice of 1 lemon
- 3 tablespoons canned chickpeas, for serving
- Parmesan shavings, for serving

1. Combine the potato, carrot, cherry tomatoes, beetroot, onion, turmeric, cumin, salt, and 1 tablespoon of olive oil in a large bowl and toss until well coated.

2. Arrange the veggies in the perforated pan.

3. Select Roast. Set temperature to 370°F (188°C) and set time to 20 minutes. Press Start to begin preheating.

4. Once preheated, place the pan into the oven. Stir the vegetables halfway through.

5. When cooking is complete, the potatoes should be golden brown.

6. Let the veggies cool for 5 to 10 minutes in the oven.

7. Put the arugula, baby spinach, lemon juice, and remaining 1 tablespoon of olive oil in a salad bowl and stir to combine. Mix in the roasted veggies and toss well.

8. Scatter the chickpeas and Parmesan shavings on top and serve immediately.

Spinach-Stuffed Beefsteak Tomatoes

Prep time: 10 minutes | Cook time: 18 minutes | Serves 4

- 4 medium beefsteak tomatoes, rinsed
- ½ cup grated carrot
- 1 medium onion, chopped
- 1 garlic clove, minced
- 2 teaspoons olive oil
- 2 cups fresh baby spinach
- ¼ cup crumbled low-sodium feta cheese
- ½ teaspoon dried basil

1. On your cutting board, cut a thin slice off the top of each tomato. Scoop out a ¼- to ½-inch-thick tomato pulp and place the tomatoes upside down on paper towels to drain. Set aside.

2. Stir together the carrot, onion, garlic, and olive oil in a baking pan.

3. Select Bake. Set temperature to 350°F (180°C) and set time

Vegan and Vegetarian

to 5 minutes. Press Start to begin preheating.

4. Once preheated, place the pan into the oven. Stir the vegetables halfway through.

5. When cooking is complete, the carrot should be crisp-tender.

6. Remove the pan from the oven and stir in the spinach, feta cheese, and basil.

7. Spoon ¼ of the vegetable mixture into each tomato and transfer the stuffed tomatoes to the oven. Set time to 13 minutes on Bake.

8. When cooking is complete, the filling should be hot and the tomatoes should be lightly caramelized.

9. Let the tomatoes cool for 5 minutes and serve.

Fast and Easy Asparagus

Prep time: 5 minutes | Cook time: 5 minutes | Serves 4

- 1 pound (454 g) fresh asparagus spears, trimmed
- 1 tablespoon olive oil
- Salt and ground black pepper, to taste

1. Place the crisper tray on the air fry position. Select Air Fry, set the temperature to 375°F (191°C), and set the time to 5 minutes.

2. Combine all the ingredients and transfer to the crisper tray.

3. Air fry for 5 minutes or until soft.

4. Serve hot.

Sriracha Golden Cauliflower

Prep time: 5 minutes | Cook time: 17 minutes | Serves 4

- ¼ cup vegan butter, melted
- ¼ cup sriracha sauce
- 4 cups cauliflower florets
- 1 cup bread crumbs
- 1 teaspoon salt

1. Place the crisper tray on the air fry position. Select Air Fry, set the temperature to 375°F (191°C), and set the time to 17 minutes.

2. Mix the sriracha and vegan butter in a bowl and pour this mixture over the cauliflower, taking care to cover each floret entirely.

3. In a separate bowl, combine the bread crumbs and salt.

4. Dip the cauliflower florets in the bread crumbs, coating each one well. Transfer to the crisper tray. Air fry for 17 minutes.

5. Serve hot.

Roasted Lemony Broccoli

Prep time: 5 minutes | Cook time: 15 minutes | Serves 6

- 2 heads broccoli, cut into florets
- 2 teaspoons extra-virgin olive oil, plus more for coating
- 1 teaspoon salt
- ½ teaspoon black pepper
- 1 clove garlic, minced
- ½ teaspoon lemon juice

1. Cover the crisper tray with aluminum foil and coat with a light brushing of oil.

2. Place the crisper tray on the roast position. Select Roast, set the temperature to 375°F (191°C), and set the time to 15 minutes.

3. In a bowl, combine all ingredients, save for the lemon juice, and transfer to the crisper tray. Roast for 15 minutes.

4. Serve with the lemon juice.

Corn Pakodas

Prep time: 10 minutes | Cook time: 8 minutes | Serves 5

- 1 cup flour
- ¼ teaspoon baking soda
- ¼ teaspoon salt
- ½ teaspoon curry powder
- ½ teaspoon red chili powder
- ¼ teaspoon turmeric powder
- ¼ cup water
- 10 cobs baby corn, blanched
- Cooking spray

1. Place the crisper tray on the air fry position. Select Air Fry, set the temperature to 425°F (218°C), and set the time to 8 minutes.

2. Cover the crisper tray with aluminum foil and spritz with the cooking spray.

3. In a bowl, combine all the ingredients, save for the corn. Stir with a whisk until well combined.

4. Coat the corn in the batter and put inside the crisper tray.

5. Air fry for 8 minutes until a golden brown color is achieved.

6. Serve hot.

Cheesy Macaroni Balls

Prep time: 10 minutes | Cook time: 10 minutes | Serves 2

- 2 cups leftover macaroni
- 1 cup shredded Cheddar cheese
- ½ cup flour
- 1 cup bread crumbs
- 3 large eggs
- 1 cup milk
- ½ teaspoon salt
- ¼ teaspoon black pepper

1. Place the crisper tray on the air fry position. Select Air Fry, set the temperature to 365°F (185°C), and set the time to 10 minutes.

2. In a bowl, combine the leftover macaroni and shredded cheese.

3. Pour the flour in a separate bowl. Put the bread crumbs in a third bowl. Finally, in a fourth bowl, mix the eggs and milk

with a whisk.

4. With an ice-cream scoop, create balls from the macaroni mixture. Coat them the flour, then in the egg mixture, and lastly in the bread crumbs.

5. Arrange the balls in the crisper tray. Air fry for 10 minutes, giving them an occasional stir. Ensure they crisp up nicely.

6. Serve hot.

Simple Pesto Gnocchi

Prep time: 10 minutes | Cook time: 15 minutes | Serves 4

- 1 (1-pound / 454-g) package gnocchi
- 1 medium onion, chopped
- 3 cloves garlic, minced
- 1 tablespoon extra-virgin
- olive oil
- 1 (8-ounce / 227-g) jar pesto
- ⅓ cup grated Parmesan cheese

1. Place the crisper tray on the air fry position. Select Air Fry, set the temperature to 340°F (171°C), and set the time to 15 minutes.

2. In a large bowl combine the onion, garlic, and gnocchi, and drizzle with the olive oil. Mix thoroughly.

3. Transfer the mixture to the crisper tray. Air fry for 15 minutes, stirring occasionally, making sure the gnocchi become light brown and crispy.

4. Add the pesto and Parmesan cheese, and give everything a good stir before serving.

Creamy Corn Casserole

Prep time: 5 minutes | Cook time: 15 minutes | Serves 4

- 2 cups frozen yellow corn
- 1 egg, beaten
- 3 tablespoons flour
- ½ cup grated Swiss or Havarti cheese
- ½ cup light cream
- ¼ cup milk
- Pinch salt
- Freshly ground black pepper, to taste
- 2 tablespoons butter, cut into cubes
- Nonstick cooking spray

1. Place the baking pan on the bake position. Select Bake, set the temperature to 320°F (160°C), and set the time to 15 minutes.

2. Spritz the baking pan with nonstick cooking spray.

3. Stir together the remaining ingredients except the butter in a medium bowl until well incorporated.

4. Transfer the mixture to the prepared baking pan and scatter with the butter cubes.

5. Bake for 15 minutes, or until the top is golden brown and a toothpick inserted in the center comes out clean.

6. Let the casserole cool for 5 minutes before slicing into

wedges and serving.

Cinnamon-Spiced Acorn Squash

Prep time: 5 minutes | Cook time: 15 minutes | Serves 2

- 1 medium acorn squash, halved crosswise and deseeded
- 1 teaspoon coconut oil
- 1 teaspoon light brown
- sugar
- Few dashes of ground cinnamon
- Few dashes of ground nutmeg

1. Place the crisper tray on the air fry position. Select Air Fry, set the temperature to 325°F (163°C), and set the time to 15 minutes.

2. On a clean work surface, rub the cut sides of the acorn squash with coconut oil. Scatter with the brown sugar, cinnamon, and nutmeg.

3. Put the squash halves in the crisper tray, cut-side up. Air fry for 15 minutes until just tender when pierced in the center with a paring knife.

4. Rest for 5 to 10 minutes and serve warm.

Charred Green Beans with Sesame Seeds

Prep time: 5 minutes | Cook time: 8 minutes | Serves 4

- 1 tablespoon reduced-sodium soy sauce or tamari
- ½ tablespoon Sriracha sauce
- 4 teaspoons toasted
- sesame oil, divided
- 12 ounces (340 g) trimmed green beans
- ½ tablespoon toasted sesame seeds

1. Place the crisper tray on the air fry position. Select Air Fry, set the temperature to 375°F (191°C), and set the time to 8 minutes.

2. Whisk together the soy sauce, Sriracha sauce, and 1 teaspoon of sesame oil in a small bowl until smooth.

3. Toss the green beans with the remaining sesame oil in a large bowl until evenly coated.

4. Place the green beans in the crisper tray in a single layer. You may need to work in batches to avoid overcrowding.

5. Air fry for 8 minutes until the green beans are lightly charred and tender. Shake the crisper tray halfway through the cooking time.

6. Remove from the crisper tray to a platter. Repeat with the remaining green beans.

7. Pour the prepared sauce over the top of green beans and toss well. Serve sprinkled with the toasted sesame seeds.

Cheesy Broccoli Gratin

Prep time: 5 minutes | Cook time: 12 to 14 minutes | Serves 2

- ⅓ cup fat-free milk
- 1 tablespoon all-purpose

Vegan and Vegetarian

- or gluten-free flour
- ½ tablespoon olive oil
- ½ teaspoon ground sage
- ¼ teaspoon kosher salt
- ⅛ teaspoon freshly ground black pepper
- 2 cups roughly chopped broccoli florets
- 6 tablespoons shredded Cheddar cheese
- 2 tablespoons panko bread crumbs
- 1 tablespoon grated Parmesan cheese
- Olive oil spray

1. Place the baking pan on the bake position. Select Bake, set the temperature to 330°F (166°C), and set the time to 14 minutes.

2. Spritz the baking pan with olive oil spray.

3. Mix the milk, flour, olive oil, sage, salt, and pepper in a medium bowl and whisk to combine. Stir in the broccoli florets, Cheddar cheese, bread crumbs, and Parmesan cheese and toss to coat.

4. Pour the broccoli mixture into the prepared baking pan.

5. Bake for 12 to 14 minutes until the top is golden brown and the broccoli is tender.

6. Serve immediately.

Baked Potatoes with Yogurt and Chives

Prep time: 5 minutes | Cook time: 35 minutes | Serves 4

- 4 (7-ounce / 198-g) russet panatoes, rinsed
- Olive oil spray
- ½ teaspoon kosher salt, divided
- ½ cup 2% plain Greek yogurt
- ¼ cup minced fresh chives
- Freshly ground black pepper, to taste

1. Place the crisper tray on the bake position. Select Bake, set the temperature to 400°F (204°C), and set the time to 35 minutes.

2. Pat the panatoes dry and pierce them all over with a fork. Spritz the panatoes with olive oil spray. Sprinkle with ¼ teaspoon of the salt.

3. Put the panatoes in the crisper tray. Bake for 35 minutes, or until a knife can be inserted into the center of the panatoes easily.

4. Remove from the crisper tray and split open the panatoes. Top with the yogurt, chives, the remaining ¼ teaspoon of salt, and finish with the black pepper. Serve immediately.

Garlic Roasted Asparagus

Prep time: 5 minutes | Cook time: 10 minutes | Serves 4

- 1 pound (454 g) asparagus, woody ends trimmed
- 2 tablespoons olive oil
- 1 tablespoon balsamic vinegar
- 2 teaspoons minced garlic
- Salt and freshly ground black pepper, to taste

1. Place the crisper tray on the roast position. Select Roast, set the temperature to 400°F (204°C), and set the time to 10 minutes.

2. In a large shallow bowl, toss the asparagus with the olive oil, balsamic vinegar, garlic, salt, and pepper until thoroughly coated.

3. Arrange the asparagus in the crisper tray. Roast for 10 minutes until crispy. Flip the asparagus with tongs halfway through the cooking time.

4. Serve warm.

Buttered Broccoli with Parmesan

Prep time: 5 minutes | Cook time: 4 minutes | Serves 4

- 1 pound (454 g) broccoli florets
- 1 medium shallot, minced
- 2 tablespoons olive oil
- 2 tablespoons unsalted
- butter, melted
- 2 teaspoons minced garlic
- ¼ cup grated Parmesan cheese

1. Place the crisper tray on the roast position. Select Roast, set the temperature to 360°F (182°C), and set the time to 4 minutes.

2. Combine the broccoli florets with the shallot, olive oil, butter, garlic, and Parmesan cheese in a medium bowl and toss until the broccoli florets are thoroughly coated.

3. Arrange the broccoli florets in the crisper tray in a single layer. Roast for 4 minutes until crisp-tender.

4. Serve warm.

Crusted Brussels Sprouts with Sage

Prep time: 5 minutes | Cook time: 15 minutes | Serves 4

- 1 pound (454 g) Brussels sprouts, halved
- 1 cup bread crumbs
- 2 tablespoons grated Grana Padano cheese
- 1 tablespoon paprika
- 2 tablespoons canola oil
- 1 tablespoon chopped sage

1. Line the crisper tray with parchment paper.

2. Place the crisper tray on the roast position. Select Roast, set the temperature to 400°F (204°C), and set the time to 15 minutes.

3. In a small bowl, thoroughly mix the bread crumbs, cheese, and paprika. In a large bowl, place the Brussels sprouts and drizzle the canola oil over the top. Sprinkle with the bread crumb mixture and toss to coat.

4. Place the Brussels sprouts in the crisper tray. Roast for 15 minutes, or until the Brussels sprouts are lightly browned and crisp. Shake the crisper tray a few times during cooking to ensure even cooking.

5. Transfer the Brussels sprouts to a plate and sprinkle the

sage on top before serving.

Spicy Cabbage

Prep time: 5 minutes | Cook time: 7 minutes | Serves 4

- 1 head cabbage, sliced into 1-inch-thick ribbons
- 1 tablespoon olive oil
- 1 teaspoon garlic powder
- 1 teaspoon red pepper flakes
- 1 teaspoon salt
- 1 teaspoon freshly ground black pepper

1. Place the crisper tray on the roast position. Select Roast, set the temperature to 350°F (177°C), and set the time to 7 minutes.

2. Toss the cabbage with the olive oil, garlic powder, red pepper flakes, salt, and pepper in a large mixing bowl until well coated.

3. Arrange the cabbage in the crisper tray. Roast for 7 minutes until crisp. Flip the cabbage with tongs halfway through the cooking time.

4. Remove from the crisper tray to a plate and serve warm.

Chapter 6 Appetizers and Snacks

Cajun Zucchini Chips

Prep time: 5 minutes | Cook time: 15 to 16 minutes | Serves 4

- 2 large zucchini, cut into ⅛-inch-thick slices
- 2 teaspoons Cajun seasoning
- Cooking spray

1. Spray the crisper tray lightly with cooking spray.

2. Place the crisper tray on the air fry position. Select Air Fry, set the temperature to 370°F (188°C), and set the time to 16 minutes.

3. Put the zucchini slices in a medium bowl and spray them generously with cooking spray.

4. Sprinkle the Cajun seasoning over the zucchini and stir to make sure they are evenly coated with oil and seasoning.

5. Place the slices in a single layer in the crisper tray, making sure not to overcrowd. You will need to cook these in several batches.

6. Air fry for 8 minutes. Flip the slices over and air fry for an additional 7 to 8 minutes, or until they are as crisp and brown as you prefer.

7. Serve immediately.

Spicy Kale Chips

Prep time: 5 minutes | Cook time: 8 to 12 minutes | Serves 4

- 5 cups kale, large stems removed and chopped
- 2 teaspoons canola oil
- ¼ teaspoon smoked
- paprika
- ¼ teaspoon kosher salt
- Cooking spray

1. Place the crisper tray on the air fry position. Select Air Fry, set the temperature to 390°F (199°C), and set the time to 6 minutes.

2. In a large bowl, toss the kale, canola oil, smoked paprika, and kosher salt.

3. Spray the crisper tray with cooking spray, then place half the kale in the crisper tray. Air fry for 2 to 3 minutes.

4. Shake the crisper tray and air fry for 2 to 3 more minutes, or until crispy. Repeat this process with the remaining kale.

5. Remove the kale and allow to cool on a wire rack for 3 to 5 minutes before serving.

Rosemary Baked Cashews

Prep time: 5 minutes | Cook time: 3 minutes | Makes 2 cups

- 2 sprigs of fresh rosemary (1 chopped and 1 whole)
- 1 teaspoon olive oil
- 1 teaspoon kosher salt
- ½ teaspoon honey
- 2 cups roasted and unsalted whole cashews
- Cooking spray

1. Place the crisper tray on the bake position. Select Bake, set the temperature to 300°F (149°C), and set the time to 3 minutes.

2. In a medium bowl, whisk together the chopped rosemary,

olive oil, kosher salt, and honey. Set aside.

3. Spray the crisper tray with cooking spray, then place the cashews and the whole rosemary sprig in the crisper tray. Bake for 3 minutes.

4. Remove the cashews and rosemary from the grill, then discard the rosemary and add the cashews to the olive oil mixture, tossing to coat.

5. Allow to cool for 15 minutes before serving.

Cayenne Sesame Nut Mix

Prep time: 10 minutes | Cook time: 2 minutes | Makes 4 cups

- 1 tablespoon buttery spread, melted
- 2 teaspoons honey
- ¼ teaspoon cayenne pepper
- 2 teaspoons sesame seeds
- ¼ teaspoon kosher salt
- ¼ teaspoon freshly ground
- black pepper
- 1 cup cashews
- 1 cup almonds
- 1 cup mini pretzels
- 1 cup rice squares cereal
- Cooking spray

1. Place the baking pan on the bake position. Select Bake, set the temperature to 360°F (182°C), and set the time to 2 minutes.

2. In a large bowl, combine the buttery spread, honey, cayenne pepper, sesame seeds, kosher salt, and black pepper, then add the cashews, almonds, pretzels, and rice squares, tossing to coat.

3. Spray the baking pan with cooking spray, then pour the mixture into the pan. Bake for 2 minutes.

4. Remove the sesame mix from the grill and allow to cool in the pan on a wire rack for 5 minutes before serving.

Crispy Prosciutto-Wrapped Asparagus

Prep time: 5 minutes | Cook time: 16 to 24 minutes | Serves 6

- 12 asparagus spears, woody ends trimmed
- 24 pieces thinly sliced
- prosciutto
- Cooking spray

1. Place the crisper tray on the air fry position. Select Air Fry, set the temperature to 360°F (182°C), and set the time to 4 minutes.

2. Wrap each asparagus spear with 2 slices of prosciutto, then repeat this process with the remaining asparagus and prosciutto.

3. Spray the crisper tray with cooking spray, then place 2 to 3 bundles in the crisper tray. Air fry for 4 minutes. Repeat this process with the remaining asparagus bundles.

4. Remove the bundles and allow to cool on a wire rack for 5 minutes before serving.

Bacon-Wrapped Dates

Prep time: 10 minutes | Cook time: 10 to 14 minutes | Serves 6

- 12 dates, pitted
- 6 slices high-quality
- bacon, cut in half
- Cooking spray

1. Place the crisper tray on the bake position. Select Bake, set the temperature to 360°F (182°C), and set the time to 7 minutes.

2. Wrap each date with half a bacon slice and secure with a toothpick.

3. Spray the crisper tray with cooking spray, then place 6 bacon-wrapped dates in the crisper tray. Bake for 5 to 7 minutes or until the bacon is crispy. Repeat this process with the remaining dates.

4. Remove the dates and allow to cool on a wire rack for 5 minutes before serving.

Caramelized Peaches

Prep time: 10 minutes | Cook time: 10 to 13 minutes | Serves 4

- 2 tablespoons sugar
- ¼ teaspoon ground cinnamon
- 4 peaches, cut into wedges
- Cooking spray

1. Lightly spray the crisper tray with cooking spray.

2. Place the crisper tray on the air fry position. Select Air Fry, set the temperature to 350°F (177°C), and set the time to 13 minutes.

3. Toss the peaches with the sugar and cinnamon in a medium bowl until evenly coated.

4. Arrange the peaches in the crisper tray in a single layer. Lightly mist the peaches with cooking spray. You may need to work in batches to avoid overcrowding.

5. Air fry for 5 minutes. Flip the peaches and air fry for another 5 to 8 minutes, or until the peaches are caramelized.

6. Repeat with the remaining peaches.

7. Let the peaches cool for 5 minutes and serve warm.

Roasted Mixed Nuts

Prep time: 5 minutes | Cook time: 20 minutes | Serves 6

- 2 cups mixed nuts (walnuts, pecans, and almonds)
- 2 tablespoons egg white
- 2 tablespoons sugar
- 1 teaspoon paprika
- 1 teaspoon ground cinnamon
- Cooking spray

1. Spray the crisper tray with cooking spray.

2. Place the crisper tray on the roast position. Select Roast, set the temperature to 300°F (149°C), and set the time to 20 minutes.

3. Stir together the mixed nuts, egg white, sugar, paprika, and cinnamon in a small bowl until the nuts are fully coated.

Appetizers and Snacks

4. Put the nuts in the crisper tray. Roast for 20 minutes. Shake the crisper tray halfway through the cooking time for even cooking.

5. Transfer the nuts to a bowl and serve warm.

Bruschetta with Tomato and Basil

Prep time: 5 minutes | Cook time: 6 minutes | Serves 6

- 4 tomatoes, diced
- ⅓ cup shredded fresh basil
- ¼ cup shredded Parmesan cheese
- 1 tablespoon balsamic vinegar
- 1 tablespoon minced garlic
- 1 teaspoon olive oil
- 1 teaspoon salt
- 1 teaspoon freshly ground black pepper
- 1 loaf French bread, cut into 1-inch-thick slices
- Cooking spray

1. Place the crisper tray on the bake position. Select Bake, set the temperature to 250°F (121°C), and set the time to 3 minutes.

2. Mix together the tomatoes and basil in a medium bowl. Add the cheese, vinegar, garlic, olive oil, salt, and pepper and stir until well incorporated. Set aside.

3. Spritz the crisper tray with cooking spray. Working in batches, lay the bread slices in the crisper tray in a single layer. Spray the slices with cooking spray.

4. Bake for 3 minutes until golden brown.

5. Remove from the crisper tray to a plate. Repeat with the remaining bread slices.

6. Top each slice with a generous spoonful of the tomato mixture and serve.

Cheesy Crab Toasts

Prep time: 10 minutes | Cook time: 5 minutes | Makes 15 to 18 toasts

- 1 (6-ounce / 170-g) can flaked crab meat, well drained
- 3 tablespoons light mayonnaise
- ¼ cup shredded Parmesan cheese
- ¼ cup shredded Cheddar
- cheese
- 1 teaspoon Worcestershire sauce
- ½ teaspoon lemon juice
- 1 loaf artisan bread, French bread, or baguette, cut into ⅜-inch-thick slices

1. Place the crisper tray on the bake position. Select Bake, set the temperature to 360°F (182°C), and set the time to 5 minutes.

2. In a large bowl, stir together all the ingredients except the bread slices.

3. On a clean work surface, lay the bread slices. Spread ½ tablespoon of crab mixture onto each slice of bread.

4. Arrange the bread slices in the crisper tray in a single layer.

You'll need to work in batches to avoid overcrowding.

5. Bake for 5 minutes until the tops are lightly browned.

6. Transfer to a plate and repeat with the remaining bread slices.

7. Serve warm.

Cuban Sandwiches

Prep time: 20 minutes | Cook time: 8 minutes | Makes 4 sandwiches

- 8 slices ciabatta bread, about ¼-inch thick
- Cooking spray
- 1 tablespoon brown mustard

Toppings:

- 6 to 8 ounces (170 to 227 g) thinly sliced leftover roast
- pork
- 4 ounces (113 g) thinly sliced deli turkey
- ⅓ cup bread and butter pickle slices
- 2 to 3 ounces (57 to 85 g) Pepper Jack cheese slices

1. Place the crisper tray on the air fry position. Select Air Fry, set the temperature to 390°F (199°C), and set the time to 8 minutes.

2. On a clean work surface, spray one side of each slice of bread with cooking spray. Spread the other side of each slice of bread evenly with brown mustard.

3. Top 4 of the bread slices with the roast pork, turkey, pickle slices, cheese, and finish with remaining bread slices. Transfer to the crisper tray.

4. Air fry for 8 minutes until golden brown.

5. Cool for 5 minutes and serve warm.

Deluxe Cheese Sandwiches

Prep time: 10 minutes | Cook time: 5 to 6 minutes | Serves 4 to 8

- 8 ounces (227 g) Brie
- 8 slices oat nut bread
- 1 large ripe pear, cored and cut into ½-inch-thick
- slices
- 2 tablespoons butter, melted

1. Place the baking pan on the bake position. Select Bake, set the temperature to 360°F (182°C), and set the time to 6 minutes. .

2. Make the sandwiches: Spread each of 4 slices of bread with ¼ of the Brie. Top the Brie with the pear slices and remaining 4 bread slices.

3. Brush the melted butter lightly on both sides of each sandwich.

4. Arrange the sandwiches in the baking pan. You may need to work in batches to avoid overcrowding.

5. Bake for 5 to 6 minutes until the cheese is melted. Repeat with the remaining sandwiches.

6. Serve warm.

Sausage and Mushroom Empanadas

Prep time: 5 minutes | Cook time: 12 minutes | Serves 4

- ½ pound (227 g) Kielbasa smoked sausage, chopped
- 4 chopped canned mushrooms
- 2 tablespoons chopped onion
- ½ teaspoon ground cumin
- ¼ teaspoon paprika
- Salt and black pepper, to taste
- ½ package puff pastry dough, at room temperature
- 1 egg, beaten
- Cooking spray

1. Spritz the crisper tray with cooking spray.
2. Place the crisper tray on the air fry position. Select Air Fry, set the temperature to 360°F (182°C), and set the time to 12 minutes.
3. Combine the sausage, mushrooms, onion, cumin, paprika, salt, and pepper in a bowl and stir to mix well.
4. Make the empanadas: Place the puff pastry dough on a lightly floured surface. Cut circles into the dough with a glass. Place 1 tablespoon of the sausage mixture into the center of each pastry circle. Fold each in half and pinch the edges to seal. Using a fork, crimp the edges. Brush them with the beaten egg and mist with cooking spray.
5. Place the empanadas in the crisper tray. Air fry for 12 minutes until golden brown. Flip the empanadas halfway through the cooking time.
6. Allow them to cool for 5 minutes and serve hot.

Homemade BBQ Chicken Pizza

Prep time: 5 minutes | Cook time: 8 minutes | Serves 1

- 1 piece naan bread
- ¼ cup Barbecue sauce
- ¼ cup shredded Monterrey Jack cheese
- ¼ cup shredded Mozzarella cheese
- ½ chicken herby sausage,
- sliced
- 2 tablespoons red onion, thinly sliced
- Chopped cilantro or parsley, for garnish
- Cooking spray

1. Place the crisper tray on the air fry position. Select Air Fry, set the temperature to 400°F (204°C), and set the time to 8 minutes.
2. Spritz the bottom of naan bread with cooking spray, then transfer to the crisper tray.
3. Brush with the Barbecue sauce. Top with the cheeses, sausage, and finish with the red onion.
4. Air fry for 8 minutes until the cheese is melted.
5. Garnish with the chopped cilantro or parsley before slicing

to serve.

Crispy Cod Fingers

Prep time: 5 minutes | Cook time: 12 minutes | Serves 4

- 2 eggs
- 2 tablespoons milk
- 2 cups flour
- 1 cup cornmeal
- 1 teaspoon seafood seasoning
- Salt and black pepper, to taste
- 1 cup bread crumbs
- 1 pound (454 g) cod fillets, cut into 1-inch strips

1. Place the crisper tray on the air fry position. Select Air Fry, set the temperature to 400°F (204°C), and set the time to 12 minutes.
2. Beat the eggs with the milk in a shallow bowl. In another shallow bowl, combine the flour, cornmeal, seafood seasoning, salt, and pepper. On a plate, place the bread crumbs.
3. Dredge the cod strips, one at a time, in the flour mixture, then in the egg mixture, finally in the bread crumb to coat evenly.
4. Arrange the cod strips in the crisper tray. Air fry for 12 minutes until crispy.
5. Transfer the cod strips to a paper towel-lined plate and serve warm.

Baked Mini Potatoes

Prep time: 15 minutes | Cook time: 20 minutes | Serves 6

- 12 small red or yellow potatoes, about 2 inches in diameter, depending on size
- 1 teaspoon kosher salt or ½ teaspoon fine salt, divided
- 1 tablespoon extra-virgin olive oil
- ¼ cup grated sharp Cheddar cheese
- ¼ cup sour cream
- 2 tablespoons chopped chives
- 2 tablespoons grated Parmesan cheese

1. Place the potatoes in a large bowl. Sprinkle with the kosher salt and drizzle with the olive oil. Toss to coat. Place the potatoes in the baking pan. Wipe out the bowl and set aside.
2. Place the pan on the roast position. Select Roast, set temperature to 375°F (191°C), and set time to 15 minutes.
3. After 10 minutes, rotate the pan 180 degrees and continue cooking.
4. When cooking is complete, check the potatoes. A sharp knife should pierce the flesh easily; if not, cook for a few more minutes. Remove the pan and let the potatoes cool until you can handle them. Halve the potatoes lengthwise. If needed, cut a small slice from the uncut side for stability. Using a small melon baller or spoon, scoop the flesh into the bowl, leaving a thin shell of skin. Place the potato

halves in the baking pan.

5. Mash the scooped-out potatoes until smooth. Add the remaining ½ teaspoon of salt, Cheddar cheese, sour cream, and chives and mix until well combined. Taste and adjust the salt, if needed. Spoon the filling into a pastry bag or heavy plastic bag with one corner snipped off. Pipe the filling into the potato shells, mounding up slightly. Sprinkle with the Parmesan cheese.

6. Place the pan on the roast position. Select Roast, set temperature to 375°F (191°C), and set time to 5 minutes.

7. When cooking is complete, the tops should be browning slightly. If necessary, cook for a couple of minutes longer. Remove the pan from the grill and let the potatoes cool slightly before serving.

Jalapeño Poppers

Prep time: 10 minutes | Cook time: 15 minutes | Serves 8

- 12 large jalapeño peppers (about 3 inches long)
- 6 ounces (170 g) cream cheese, at room temperature
- 1 teaspoon chili powder
- 4 ounces (113 g) shredded Cheddar cheese
- 2 slices cooked bacon, chopped fine
- ¼ cup panko bread crumbs
- 1 tablespoon butter, melted

1. If the jalapeños have stems, cut them off flush with the tops of the chiles. Slice the jalapeños in half lengthwise and scoop out the seeds. For milder poppers, remove the white membranes (the ribs). (You should probably wear latex gloves when you do this, to avoid possible burns. I often forget, and I often regret it.)

2. In a medium bowl, mix the cream cheese, chili powder, and Cheddar cheese. Spoon the cheese mixture into the jalapeño halves and place them in the baking pan. If the jalapeños roll or tip, use a vegetable peeler to scrape away a thin layer of skin on the base so they're more stable.

3. In a small bowl, stir together the bacon, panko, and butter. Top each of the jalapeño halves with the panko mixture.

4. Place the pan on the roast position. Select Roast, set temperature to 375°F (191°C), and set time to 15 minutes.

5. After 7 or 8 minutes, rotate the pan 180 degrees and continue cooking until the peppers have softened somewhat, the filling is bubbling, and the panko is browned.

6. When cooking is complete, remove the pan from the grill. Let the poppers cool for a few minutes before serving.

Chapter 7 Desserts

Ultimate Skillet Brownies

Prep time: 15 minutes | Cook time: 40 minutes | Serves 6

- ½ cup all-purpose flour
- ¼ cup unsweetened cocoa powder
- ¾ teaspoon sea salt
- 2 large eggs
- 1 tablespoon water
- ½ cup granulated sugar
- ½ cup dark brown sugar
- 1 tablespoon vanilla extract
- 8 ounces (227 g) semisweet chocolate chips, melted
- ¾ cup unsalted butter, melted
- Nonstick cooking spray

1. In a medium bowl, whisk together the flour, cocoa powder, and salt.

2. In a large bowl, whisk together the eggs, water, sugar, brown sugar, and vanilla until smooth.

3. In a microwave-safe bowl, melt the chocolate in the microwave. In a separate microwave-safe bowl, melt the butter.

4. In a separate medium bowl, stir together the chocolate and butter until evenly combined. Whisk into the egg mixture. Then slowly add the dry ingredients, stirring just until incorporated.

5. Place the baking pan on the bake position. Select Bake, set the temperature to 350°F (177°C), and set the time to 40 minutes.

6. Lightly grease the baking pan with cooking spray. Pour the batter into the pan, spreading evenly.

7. Bake for 40 minutes.

8. After 40 minutes, check that baking is complete. A wooden toothpick inserted into the center of the brownies should come out clean.

Simple Corn Biscuits

Prep time: 15 minutes | Cook time: 15 minutes | Serves 6

- 1½ cups all-purpose flour, plus additional for dusting
- ½ cup yellow cornmeal
- 2½ teaspoons baking powder
- ½ teaspoon sea salt
- ⅓ cup vegetable shortening
- ⅔ cup buttermilk
- Nonstick cooking spray

1. In a large bowl, combine the flour, cornmeal, baking powder, and salt.

2. Add the shortening, and cut it into the flour mixture, until well combined and the dough resembles a coarse meal. Add the buttermilk and stir together just until moistened.

3. Place the crisper tray on the air fry position. Select Air Fry, set the temperature to 350°F (177°C), and set the time to 15 minutes.

4. Dust a clean work surface with flour. Knead the mixture on the floured surface until a cohesive dough forms. Roll out the dough to an even thickness, then cut into biscuits with a 2-inch biscuit cutter.

5. Coat the crisper tray with cooking spray. Place 6 to 8 biscuits in the crisper tray, well spaced, and spray each with cooking spray. Air fry for 12 to 15 minutes, until golden brown.

6. Gently remove the biscuits from the crisper tray, and place them on a wire rack to cool. Repeat with the remaining dough.

Oatmeal and Carrot Cookie Cups

Prep time: 10 minutes | Cook time: 8 minutes | Makes 16 cups

- 3 tablespoons unsalted butter, at room temperature
- ¼ cup packed brown sugar
- 1 tablespoon honey
- 1 egg white
- ½ teaspoon vanilla extract
- ⅓ cup finely grated carrot
- ½ cup quick-cooking oatmeal
- ⅓ cup whole-wheat pastry flour
- ½ teaspoon baking soda
- ¼ cup dried cherries

1. Place the baking pan on the bake position. Select Bake, set the temperature to 350°F (177°C), and set the time to 8 minutes.

2. In a medium bowl, beat the butter, brown sugar, and honey until well combined.

3. Add the egg white, vanilla, and carrot. Beat to combine.

4. Stir in the oatmeal, pastry flour, and baking soda.

5. Stir in the dried cherries.

6. Double up 32 mini muffin foil cups to make 16 cups. Fill each with about 4 teaspoons of dough. Place the cookie cups directly in the pan.

7. Bake for 8 minutes, 8 at a time, or until light golden brown and just set. Serve warm.

Curry Peaches, Pears, and Plums

Prep time: 5 minutes | Cook time: 5 minutes | Serves 6 to 8

- 2 peaches
- 2 firm pears
- 2 plums
- 2 tablespoons melted
- butter
- 1 tablespoon honey
- 2 to 3 teaspoons curry powder

1. Place the crisper tray on the bake position. Select Bake, set the temperature to 325°F (163°C), and set the time to 8 minutes.

2. Cut the peaches in half, remove the pits, and cut each half in half again. Cut the pears in half, core them, and remove the stem. Cut each half in half again. Do the same with the plums.

3. Spread a large sheet of heavy-duty foil on the work surface. Arrange the fruit on the foil and drizzle with the butter and honey. Sprinkle with the curry powder.

4. Wrap the fruit in the foil, making sure to leave some air space in the packet.

5. Put the foil package in the crisper tray. Bake for 5 to 8 minutes, shaking the crisper tray once during the cooking time, until the fruit is soft.

6. Serve immediately.

Apple, Peach, and Cranberry Crisp

Prep time: 10 minutes | Cook time: 12 minutes | Serves 8

- 1 apple, peeled and chopped
- 2 peaches, peeled and chopped
- ⅓ cup dried cranberries
- 2 tablespoons honey
- ⅓ cup brown sugar
- ¼ cup flour
- ½ cup oatmeal
- 3 tablespoons softened butter

1. Place the baking pan on the bake position. Select Bake, set the temperature to 370°F (188°C), and set the time to 12 minutes.

2. In the baking pan, combine the apple, peaches, cranberries, and honey, and mix well.

3. In a medium bowl, combine the brown sugar, flour, oatmeal, and butter, and mix until crumbly. Sprinkle this mixture over the fruit in the pan.

4. Bake for 10 to 12 minutes or until the fruit is bubbly and the topping is golden brown. Serve warm.

Orange Cake

Prep time: 10 minutes | Cook time: 23 minutes | Serves 8

- Nonstick baking spray with flour
- 1¼ cups all-purpose flour
- ⅓ cup yellow cornmeal
- ¾ cup white sugar
- 1 teaspoon baking soda
- ¼ cup safflower oil
- 1¼ cups orange juice, divided
- 1 teaspoon vanilla
- ¼ cup powdered sugar

1. Place the baking pan on the bake position. Select Bake, set the temperature to 350°F (177°C), and set the time to 23 minutes.

2. Spray the baking pan with nonstick spray and set aside.

3. In a medium bowl, combine the flour, cornmeal, sugar, baking soda, safflower oil, 1 cup of the orange juice, and vanilla, and mix well.

4. Pour the batter into the baking pan. Bake for 23 minutes or until a toothpick inserted in the center of the cake comes out clean.

5. Remove the cake from the grill and place on a cooling rack. Using a toothpick, make about 20 holes in the cake.

6. In a small bowl, combine remaining ¼ cup of orange juice

and the powdered sugar and stir well. Drizzle this mixture over the hot cake slowly so the cake absorbs it.

7. Cool completely, then cut into wedges to serve.

Black Forest Pies

Prep time: 10 minutes | Cook time: 15 minutes | Serves 6

- 3 tablespoons milk or dark chocolate chips
- 2 tablespoons thick, hot fudge sauce
- 2 tablespoons chopped dried cherries
- 1 (10-by-15-inch) sheet frozen puff pastry, thawed
- 1 egg white, beaten
- 2 tablespoons sugar
- ½ teaspoon cinnamon

1. Place the crisper tray on the bake position. Select Bake, set the temperature to 350°F (177°C), and set the time to 15 minutes.

2. In a small bowl, combine the chocolate chips, fudge sauce, and dried cherries.

3. Roll out the puff pastry on a floured surface. Cut into 6 squares with a sharp knife.

4. Divide the chocolate chip mixture into the center of each puff pastry square. Fold the squares in half to make triangles. Firmly press the edges with the tines of a fork to seal.

5. Brush the triangles on all sides sparingly with the beaten egg white. Sprinkle the tops with sugar and cinnamon.

6. Put in the crisper tray. Bake for 15 minutes or until the triangles are golden brown. The filling will be hot, so cool for at least 20 minutes before serving.

Apple Bake with Cinnamon

Prep time: 15 minutes | Cook time: 12 minutes | Serves 4

- 1 cup packed light brown sugar
- 2 teaspoons ground
- cinnamon
- 2 medium Granny Smith apples, peeled and diced

1. Thoroughly combine the brown sugar and cinnamon in a medium bowl.

2. Add the apples to the bowl and stir until well coated. Transfer the apples to a baking pan.

3. Select Bake. Set temperature to 350°F (180°C) and set time to 12 minutes. Press Start to begin preheating.

4. Once the oven has preheated, place the pan into the oven.

5. After about 9 minutes, stir the apples and bake for an additional 3 minutes. When cooking is complete, the apples should be softened.

6. Serve warm.

Vanilla Fudge Pie

Prep time: 15 minutes | Cook time: 26 minutes | Serves 8

- 1½ cups sugar
- ½ cup self-rising flour
- ⅓ cup unsweetened cocoa powder
- 3 large eggs, beaten
- 12 tablespoons (1½ sticks)
- butter, melted
- 1½ teaspoons vanilla extract
- 1 (9-inch) unbaked pie crust
- ¼ cup confectioners' sugar (optional)

1. Thoroughly combine the sugar, flour, and cocoa powder in a medium bowl. Add the beaten eggs and butter and whisk to combine. Stir in the vanilla.

2. Pour the prepared filling into the pie crust and transfer to the perforated pan.

3. Select Bake. Set temperature to 350°F (180°C) and set time to 26 minutes. Press Start to begin preheating.

4. Once the oven has preheated, place the pan into the oven.

5. When cooking is complete, the pie should be set.

6. Allow the pie to cool for 5 minutes. Sprinkle with the confectioners' sugar, if desired. Serve warm.

Chocolate Cake with Blackberries

Prep time: 10 minutes | Cook time: 22 minutes | Serves 8

- ½ cup butter, at room temperature
- 2 ounces (57 g) Swerve
- 4 eggs
- 1 cup almond flour
- 1 teaspoon baking soda
- ⅓ teaspoon baking powder
- ½ cup cocoa powder
- 1 teaspoon orange zest
- ⅓ cup fresh blackberries

1. With an electric mixer or hand mixer, beat the butter and Swerve until creamy.

2. One at a time, mix in the eggs and beat again until fluffy.

3. Add the almond flour, baking soda, baking powder, cocoa powder, orange zest and mix well. Add the butter mixture to the almond flour mixture and stir until well blended. Fold in the blackberries.

4. Scrape the batter into a baking pan.

5. Select Bake. Set temperature to 335°F (168°C) and set time to 22 minutes. Press Start to begin preheating.

6. Once the oven has preheated, place the pan into the oven.

7. When cooking is complete, a toothpick inserted into the center of the cake should come out clean.

8. Allow the cake cool on a wire rack to room temperature. Serve immediately.

Blackberry Cobbler

Prep time: 15 minutes | Cook time: 20 to 25 minutes | Serves 6

- 3 cups fresh or frozen
- blackberries

- 1¾ cups sugar, divided
- 1 teaspoon vanilla extract
- 8 tablespoons (1 stick)
- butter, melted
- 1 cup self-rising flour
- Cooking spray

1. Spritz a baking pan with cooking spray.

2. Mix the blackberries, 1 cup of sugar, and vanilla in a medium bowl and stir to combine.

3. Stir together the melted butter, remaining sugar, and flour in a separate medium bowl.

4. Spread the blackberry mixture evenly in the prepared pan and top with the butter mixture.

5. Select Bake. Set temperature to 350°F (180°C) and set time to 25 minutes. Press Start to begin preheating.

6. Once the oven has preheated, place the pan into the oven.

7. After about 20 minutes, check if the cobbler has a golden crust and you can't see any batter bubbling while it cooks. If needed, bake for another 5 minutes.

8. Remove from the oven and place on a wire rack to cool to room temperature. Serve immediately.

Chocolate Chip Brownies

Prep time: 10 minutes | Cook time: 20 minutes | Makes 1 dozen brownies

- 1 egg
- ¼ cup brown sugar
- 2 tablespoons white sugar
- 2 tablespoons safflower oil
- 1 teaspoon vanilla
- ⅓ cup all-purpose flour
- ¼ cup cocoa powder
- ¼ cup white chocolate chips
- Nonstick cooking spray

1. Spritz a baking pan with nonstick cooking spray.

2. Whisk together the egg, brown sugar, and white sugar in a medium bowl. Mix in the safflower oil and vanilla and stir to combine.

3. Add the flour and cocoa powder and stir just until incorporated. Fold in the white chocolate chips.

4. Scrape the batter into the prepared baking pan.

5. Select Bake. Set temperature to 340°F (171°C) and set time to 20 minutes. Press Start to begin preheating.

6. Once the oven has preheated, place the pan into the oven.

7. When done, the brownie should spring back when touched lightly with your fingers.

8. Transfer to a wire rack and let cool for 30 minutes before slicing to serve.

White Chocolate Cookies with Nutmeg

Prep time: 5 minutes | Cook time: 11 minutes | Serves 10

- 8 ounces (227 g) unsweetened white
- chocolate

- 2 eggs, well beaten
- ¾ cup butter, at room temperature
- 1⅔ cups almond flour
- ½ cup coconut flour
- ¾ cup granulated Swerve
- 2 tablespoons coconut oil
- ⅓ teaspoon grated nutmeg
- ⅓ teaspoon ground allspice
- ⅓ teaspoon ground anise star
- ¼ teaspoon fine sea salt

1. Line a baking sheet with parchment paper.

2. Combine all the ingredients in a mixing bowl and knead for about 3 to 4 minutes, or until a soft dough forms. Transfer to the refrigerator to chill for 20 minutes.

3. Make the cookies: Roll the dough into 1-inch balls and transfer to the parchment-lined baking sheet, spacing 2 inches apart. Flatten each with the back of a spoon.

4. Select Bake. Set temperature to 350°F (180°C) and set time to 11 minutes. Press Start to begin preheating.

5. Once the oven has preheated, place the baking sheet into the oven.

6. When cooking is complete, the cookies should be golden and firm to the touch.

7. Transfer to a wire rack and let the cookies cool completely. Serve immediately.

Peanut Butter Bread Pudding

Prep time: 10 minutes | Cook time: 10 minutes | Serves 8

- 1 egg
- 1 egg yolk
- ¾ cup chocolate milk
- 3 tablespoons brown sugar
- 3 tablespoons peanut butter
- 2 tablespoons cocoa powder
- 1 teaspoon vanilla
- 5 slices firm white bread, cubed
- Nonstick cooking spray

1. Spritz a baking pan with nonstick cooking spray.

2. Whisk together the egg, egg yolk, chocolate milk, brown sugar, peanut butter, cocoa powder, and vanilla until well combined.

3. Fold in the bread cubes and stir to mix well. Allow the bread soak for 10 minutes.

4. When ready, transfer the egg mixture to the prepared baking pan.

5. Select Bake. Set temperature to 330°F (166°C) and set time to 10 minutes. Press Start to begin preheating.

6. Once the oven has preheated, place the pan into the oven.

7. When done, the pudding should be just firm to the touch.

8. Serve at room temperature.

Cinnamon Pineapple Rings

Prep time: 5 minutes | Cook time: 7 minutes | Serves 6

- 1 cup rice milk
- ⅔ cup flour
- ½ cup water
- ¼ cup unsweetened flaked coconut
- 4 tablespoons sugar
- ½ teaspoon baking soda
- ½ teaspoon baking powder
- ½ teaspoon vanilla essence
- ½ teaspoon ground cinnamon
- ¼ teaspoon ground anise star
- Pinch of kosher salt
- 1 medium pineapple, peeled and sliced

1. In a large bowl, stir together all the ingredients except the pineapple.

2. Dip each pineapple slice into the batter until evenly coated.

3. Arrange the pineapple slices in the perforated pan.

4. Select Air Fry. Set temperature to 380°F (193°C) and set time to 7 minutes. Press Start to begin preheating.

5. Once the oven has preheated, place the pan into the oven.

6. When cooking is complete, the pineapple rings should be golden brown.

7. Remove from the oven to a plate and cool for 5 minutes before serving.

Mixed Berry Crisp with Cloves

Prep time: 5 minutes | Cook time: 20 minutes | Serves 6

- 1 tablespoon butter, melted
- 12 ounces (340 g) mixed berries
- ⅓ cup granulated Swerve
- 1 teaspoon pure vanilla extract
- ½ teaspoon ground cinnamon
- ¼ teaspoon ground cloves
- ¼ teaspoon grated nutmeg
- ½ cup coconut chips, for garnish

1. Coat a baking pan with melted butter.

2. Put the remaining ingredients except the coconut chips in the prepared baking pan.

3. Select Bake. Set temperature to 330°F (166°C) and set time to 20 minutes. Press Start to begin preheating.

4. Once the oven has preheated, place the pan into the oven.

5. When cooking is complete, remove from the oven. Serve garnished with the coconut chips.

Pineapple Sticks with Coconut

Prep time: 10 minutes | Cook time: 10 minutes | Serves 4

- ½ fresh pineapple, cut into sticks
- ¼ cup desiccated coconut

1. Place the desiccated coconut on a plate and roll the pineapple sticks in the coconut until well coated.

2. Lay the pineapple sticks in the perforated pan.

3. Select Air Fry. Set temperature to 400°F (205°C) and set time to 10 minutes. Press Start to begin preheating.

4. Once the oven has preheated, place the pan into the oven.

5. When cooking is complete, the pineapple sticks should be crisp-tender.

6. Serve warm.

Chocolate S'mores

Prep time: 5 minutes | Cook time: 3 minutes | Makes 12 s'mores

- 12 whole cinnamon graham crackers, halved
- 2 (1.55-ounce / 44-g)
- chocolate bars, cut into 12 pieces
- 12 marshmallows

1. Arrange 12 graham cracker squares in the perforated pan in a single layer.

2. Top each square with a piece of chocolate.

3. Select Bake. Set temperature to 350°F (180°C) and set time to 3 minutes. Press Start to begin preheating.

4. Once the oven has preheated, place the pan into the oven.

5. After 2 minutes, remove the pan and place a marshmallow on each piece of melted chocolate. Return the pan to the oven and continue to cook for another 1 minute.

6. Remove from the oven to a serving plate.

7. Serve topped with the remaining graham cracker squares

Pecan Pie with Chocolate Chips

Prep time: 20 minutes | Cook time: 25 minutes | Serves 8

- 1 (9-inch) unbaked pie crust

Filling:

- 2 large eggs
- ⅓ cup butter, melted
- 1 cup sugar
- ½ cup all-purpose flour
- 1 cup milk chocolate chips
- 1½ cups coarsely chopped pecans
- 2 tablespoons bourbon

1. Whisk the eggs and melted butter in a large bowl until creamy.

2. Add the sugar and flour and stir to incorporate. Mix in the milk chocolate chips, pecans, and bourbon and stir until well combined.

3. Use a fork to prick holes in the bottom and sides of the pie crust. Pour the prepared filling into the pie crust. Place the pie crust in the perforated pan.

4. Select Bake. Set temperature to 350°F (180°C) and set time to 25 minutes. Press Start to begin preheating.

5. Once the oven has preheated, place the pan into the oven.

6. When cooking is complete, a toothpick inserted in the center should come out clean.

7. Allow the pie cool for 10 minutes in the pan before serving.

Vanilla Baked Peaches and Blueberries

Prep time: 10 minutes | Cook time: 10 minutes | Serves 6

- 3 peaches, peeled, halved, and pitted
- 2 tablespoons packed brown sugar
- 1 cup plain Greek yogurt
- ¼ teaspoon ground cinnamon
- 1 teaspoon pure vanilla extract
- 1 cup fresh blueberries

1. Arrange the peaches in the perforated pan, cut-side up. Top with a generous sprinkle of brown sugar.

2. Select Bake. Set temperature to 380°F (193°C) and set time to 10 minutes. Press Start to begin preheating.

3. Once the oven has preheated, place the pan into the oven.

4. Meanwhile, whisk together the yogurt, cinnamon, and vanilla in a small bowl until smooth.

5. When cooking is complete, the peaches should be lightly browned and caramelized.

6. Remove the peaches from the oven to a plate. Serve topped with the yogurt mixture and fresh blueberries.

Graham Cracker Cheesecake

Prep time: 10 minutes | Cook time: 20 minutes | Serves 8

- 1 cup graham cracker crumbs
- 3 tablespoons softened butter
- 1½ (8-ounce / 227-g) packages cream cheese, softened
- ⅓ cup sugar
- 2 eggs
- 1 tablespoon flour
- 1 teaspoon vanilla
- ¼ cup chocolate syrup

1. For the crust, combine the graham cracker crumbs and butter in a small bowl and mix well. Press into the bottom of the baking pan and put in the freezer to set.

2. For the filling, combine the cream cheese and sugar in a medium bowl and mix well. Beat in the eggs, one at a time. Add the flour and vanilla.

3. Place the baking pan on the bake position. Select Bake, set the temperature to 450°F (232°C), and set the time to 20 minutes.

4. Remove ⅔ cup of the filling to a small bowl and stir in the chocolate syrup until combined.

5. Pour the vanilla filling into the pan with the crust. Drop the chocolate filling over the vanilla filling by the spoonful. With a clean butter knife, stir the fillings in a zigzag pattern to marbleize them.

6. Bake for 20 minutes or until the cheesecake is just set.

7. Cool on a wire rack for 1 hour, then chill in the refrigerator until the cheesecake is firm.

8. Serve immediately.

Chocolate and Peanut Butter Lava Cupcakes

Prep time: 10 minutes | Cook time: 10 to 13 minutes | Serves 8

- Nonstick baking spray with flour
- 1⅓ cups chocolate cake mix
- 1 egg
- 1 egg yolk
- ¼ cup safflower oil
- ¼ cup hot water
- ⅓ cup sour cream
- 3 tablespoons peanut butter
- 1 tablespoon powdered sugar

1. Place the baking pan on the bake position. Select Bake, set the temperature to 350°F (177°C), and set the time to 13 minutes.

2. Double up 16 foil muffin cups to make 8 cups. Spray each lightly with nonstick spray; set aside.

3. In a medium bowl, combine the cake mix, egg, egg yolk, safflower oil, water, and sour cream, and beat until combined.

4. In a small bowl, combine the peanut butter and powdered sugar and mix well. Form this mixture into 8 balls.

5. Spoon about ¼ cup of the chocolate batter into each muffin cup and top with a peanut butter ball. Spoon remaining batter on top of the peanut butter balls to cover them.

6. Arrange the cups in the pan, leaving some space between each. Bake for 10 to 13 minutes or until the tops look dry and set.

7. Let the cupcakes cool for about 10 minutes, then serve warm.

Rich Chocolate Cookie

Prep time: 10 minutes | Cook time: 9 minutes | Serves 4

- Nonstick baking spray with flour
- 3 tablespoons softened butter
- ⅓ cup plus 1 tablespoon brown sugar
- 1 egg yolk
- ½ cup flour
- 2 tablespoons ground white chocolate
- ¼ teaspoon baking soda
- ½ teaspoon vanilla
- ¾ cup chocolate chips

1. Place the baking pan on the bake position. Select Bake, set the temperature to 350°F (177°C), and set the time to 9 minutes.

2. In a medium bowl, beat the butter and brown sugar together until fluffy. Stir in the egg yolk.

3. Add the flour, white chocolate, baking soda, and vanilla, and mix well. Stir in the chocolate chips.

4. Line the baking pan with parchment paper. Spray the parchment paper with nonstick baking spray with flour.

5. Spread the batter into the prepared pan, leaving a ½-inch border on all sides.

6. Bake for 9 minutes or until the cookie is light brown and just barely set.

7. Remove the pan from the grill and let cool for 10 minutes. Remove the cookie from the pan, remove the parchment paper, and let cool on a wire rack.

8. Serve immediately.

Lemony Blackberry Crisp

Prep time: 5 minutes | Cook time: 20 minutes | Serves 1

- 2 tablespoons lemon juice
- 2 cup blackberries
- ⅓ cup powdered erythritol
- 1 cup crunchy granola
- ¼ teaspoon xantham gum

1. Place the baking pan on the bake position. Select Bake, set the temperature to 350°F (177°C), and set the time to 15 minutes.

2. In a bowl, combine the lemon juice, erythritol, xantham gum, and blackberries. Transfer to the baking pan and cover with aluminum foil.

3. Bake for 12 minutes.

4. Take care when removing the pan from the grill. Give the blackberries a stir and top with the granola.

5. Return the pan to the grill and bake at 320°F (160°C) for an additional 3 minutes. Serve once the granola has turned brown and enjoy.

Pumpkin Pudding

Prep time: 10 minutes | Cook time: 15 minutes | Serves 4

- 3 cups pumpkin purée
- 1 teaspoon nutmeg
- 3 tablespoons honey
- 1 cup full-fat cream
- 1 tablespoon ginger
- 2 eggs
- 1 tablespoon cinnamon
- 1 cup sugar
- 1 teaspoon clove

1. Place the baking pan on the bake position. Select Bake, set the temperature to 390°F (199°C), and set the time to 15 minutes.

2. In a bowl, stir all the ingredients together to combine.

3. Scrape the mixture into the greased baking pan. Bake for 15 minutes.

4. Serve warm.

Banana and Walnut Cake

Prep time: 10 minutes | Cook time: 25 minutes | Serves 6

- 1 pound (454 g) bananas, mashed
- 8 ounces (227 g) flour
- 6 ounces (170 g) sugar

- 3.5 ounces (99 g) walnuts, chopped
- melted
- 2 eggs, lightly beaten
- 2.5 ounces (71 g) butter,
- ¼ teaspoon baking soda

1. Place the baking pan on the bake position. Select Bake, set the temperature to 355°F (179°C), and set the time to 10 minutes.

2. In a bowl, combine the sugar, butter, egg, flour, and baking soda with a whisk. Stir in the bananas and walnuts.

3. Transfer the mixture to the greased baking pan. Bake for 10 minutes.

4. Reduce the temperature to 330°F (166°C) and bake for another 15 minutes. Serve hot.

Pineapple and Chocolate Cake

Prep time: 10 minutes | Cook time: 35 to 40 minutes | Serves 4

- 2 cups flour
- ½ cup pineapple juice
- 4 ounces (113 g) butter, melted
- 1 ounce (28 g) dark chocolate, grated
- ¼ cup sugar
- 1 large egg
- ½ pound (227 g) pineapple, chopped
- 2 tablespoons skimmed milk

1. Grease a cake tin with a little oil or butter.

2. Place the cake tin on the bake position. Select Bake, set the temperature to 370°F (188°C), and set the time to 40 minutes.

3. In a bowl, combine the butter and flour to create a crumbly consistency.

4. Add the sugar, chopped pineapple, juice, and grated dark chocolate and mix well.

5. In a separate bowl, combine the egg and milk. Add this mixture to the flour mixture and stir well until a soft dough forms.

6. Pour the mixture into the cake tin and transfer to the grill.

7. Bake for 35 to 40 minutes.

8. Serve immediately.

Chocolate Molten Cake

Prep time: 5 minutes | Cook time: 10 minutes | Serves 4

- 3.5 ounces (99 g) butter, melted
- chocolate, melted
- 1½ tablespoons flour
- 3½ tablespoons sugar
- 2 eggs
- 3.5 ounces (99 g)

1. Place the baking pan on the bake position. Select Bake, set the temperature to 375°F (191°C), and set the time to 10 minutes.

2. Grease four ramekins with a little butter.

3. Rigorously combine the eggs, butter, and sugar before stirring in the melted chocolate.

4. Slowly fold in the flour.

5. Spoon an equal amount of the mixture into each ramekin.

6. Put them in the pan. Bake for 10 minutes.

7. Put the ramekins upside-down on plates and let the cakes fall out. Serve hot.

Pear and Apple Crisp

Prep time: 10 minutes | Cook time: 20 minutes | Serves 6

- ½ pound (227 g) apples, cored and chopped
- ½ pound (227 g) pears, cored and chopped
- 1 cup flour
- 1 cup sugar
- 1 tablespoon butter
- 1 teaspoon ground cinnamon
- ¼ teaspoon ground cloves
- 1 teaspoon vanilla extract
- ¼ cup chopped walnuts
- Whipped cream, for serving

1. Place the baking pan on the bake position. Select Bake, set the temperature to 340°F (171°C), and set the time to 20 minutes.

2. Lightly grease the baking pan and place the apples and pears inside.

3. Combine the rest of the ingredients, minus the walnuts and the whipped cream, until a coarse, crumbly texture is achieved.

4. Pour the mixture over the fruits and spread it evenly. Top with the chopped walnuts.

5. Bake for 20 minutes or until the top turns golden brown.

6. Serve at room temperature with whipped cream.

Chocolate Coconut Brownies

Prep time: 15 minutes | Cook time: 15 minutes | Serves 8

- ½ cup coconut oil
- 2 ounces (57 g) dark chocolate
- 1 cup sugar
- 2½ tablespoons water
- 4 whisked eggs
- ¼ teaspoon ground cinnamon
- ½ teaspoons ground anise
- star
- ¼ teaspoon coconut extract
- ½ teaspoons vanilla extract
- 1 tablespoon honey
- ½ cup flour
- ½ cup desiccated coconut
- Sugar, for dusting

1. Place the baking pan on the bake position. Select Bake, set the temperature to 355°F (179°C), and set the time to 15 minutes.

2. Melt the coconut oil and dark chocolate in the microwave.

3. Combine with the sugar, water, eggs, cinnamon, anise, coconut extract, vanilla, and honey in a large bowl.

4. Stir in the flour and desiccated coconut. Incorporate everything well.

5. Lightly grease the baking pan with butter. Transfer the mixture to the pan.

6. Bake for 15 minutes.

7. Remove from the grill and allow to cool slightly.

8. Take care when taking it out of the baking pan. Slice it into squares.

9. Dust with sugar before serving.

Chocolate and Coconut Cake

Prep time: 5 minutes | Cook time: 15 minutes | Serves 6

- ½ cup unsweetened chocolate, chopped
- ½ stick butter, at room temperature
- 1 tablespoon liquid stevia
- 1½ cups coconut flour
- 2 eggs, whisked
- ½ teaspoon vanilla extract
- A pinch of fine sea salt
- Cooking spray

1. Place the chocolate, butter, and stevia in a microwave-safe bowl. Microwave for about 30 seconds until melted.

2. Let the chocolate mixture cool for 5 to 10 minutes.

3. Add the remaining ingredients to the bowl of chocolate mixture and whisk to incorporate.

4. Place the baking pan on the bake position. Select Bake, set the temperature to 330°F (166°C), and set the time to 15 minutes.

5. Lightly spray the baking pan with cooking spray.

6. Scrape the chocolate mixture into the prepared baking pan.

7. Bake for 15 minutes, or until the top springs back lightly when gently pressed with your fingers.

8. Let the cake cool for 5 minutes and serve.

Orange Coconut Cake

Prep time: 5 minutes | Cook time: 17 minutes | Serves 6

- 1 stick butter, melted
- ¾ cup granulated Swerve
- 2 eggs, beaten
- ¾ cup coconut flour
- ¼ teaspoon salt
- ⅓ teaspoon grated nutmeg
- ⅓ cup coconut milk
- 1¼ cups almond flour
- ½ teaspoon baking powder
- 2 tablespoons unsweetened orange jam
- Cooking spray

1. Place the baking pan on the bake position. Select Bake, set the temperature to 355°F (179°C), and set the time to 17 minutes.

2. Coat the baking pan with cooking spray. Set aside.

3. In a large mixing bowl, whisk together the melted butter and granulated Swerve until fluffy.

4. Mix in the beaten eggs and whisk again until smooth. Stir in the coconut flour, salt, and nutmeg and gradually pour in the coconut milk. Add the remaining ingredients and stir until well incorporated.

5. Scrape the batter into the baking pan.

6. Bake for 17 minutes until the top of the cake springs back when gently pressed with your fingers.

7. Remove from the grill to a wire rack to cool. Serve chilled.

Coffee Chocolate Cake

Prep time: 5 minutes | Cook time: 30 minutes | Serves 8

Dry Ingredients:

- 1½ cups almond flour
- ½ cup coconut meal
- ⅔ cup Swerve
- 1 teaspoon baking powder
- ¼ teaspoon salt

Wet Ingredients:

- 1 egg
- 1 stick butter, melted
- ½ cup hot strongly brewed coffee

Topping:

- ½ cup confectioner's Swerve
- ¼ cup coconut flour
- 3 tablespoons coconut oil
- 1 teaspoon ground cinnamon
- ½ teaspoon ground cardamom

1. Place the baking pan on the bake position. Select Bake, set the temperature to 330°F (166°C), and set the time to 30 minutes.

2. In a medium bowl, combine the almond flour, coconut meal, Swerve, baking powder, and salt.

3. In a large bowl, whisk the egg, melted butter, and coffee until smooth.

4. Add the dry mixture to the wet and stir until well incorporated. Transfer the batter to the greased baking pan.

5. Stir together all the ingredients for the topping in a small bowl. Spread the topping over the batter and smooth the top with a spatula.

6. Bake for 30 minutes, or until the cake springs back when gently pressed with your fingers.

7. Rest for 10 minutes before serving.

Ultimate Coconut Chocolate Cake

Prep time: 5 minutes | Cook time: 15 minutes | Serves 10

- 1¼ cups unsweetened bakers' chocolate
- 1 stick butter
- 1 teaspoon liquid stevia
- ⅓ cup shredded coconut
- 2 tablespoons coconut milk
- 2 eggs, beaten
- Cooking spray

1. Place the baking pan on the bake position. Select Bake, set the temperature to 330°F (166°C), and set the time to 15 minutes.

2. Lightly spritz the baking pan with cooking spray.

3. Place the chocolate, butter, and stevia in a microwave-safe bowl. Microwave for about 30 seconds until melted. Let the chocolate mixture cool to room temperature.

4. Add the remaining ingredients to the chocolate mixture and stir until well incorporated. Pour the batter into the prepared baking pan.

5. Bake for 15 minutes, or until a toothpick inserted in the center comes out clean.

6. Remove from the pan and allow to cool for about 10 minutes before serving.

Orange and Anise Cake

Prep time: 5 minutes | Cook time: 20 minutes | Serves 6

- 1 stick butter, at room temperature
- 5 tablespoons liquid monk fruit
- 2 eggs plus 1 egg yolk, beaten
- ⅓ cup hazelnuts, roughly chopped
- 3 tablespoons sugar-free orange marmalade
- 6 ounces (170 g) unbleached almond flour
- 1 teaspoon baking soda
- ½ teaspoon baking powder
- ½ teaspoon ground cinnamon
- ½ teaspoon ground allspice
- ½ ground anise seed
- Cooking spray

1. Place the baking pan on the bake position. Select Bake, set the temperature to 310°F (154°C), and set the time to 20 minutes.

2. Lightly spritz the baking pan with cooking spray.

3. In a mixing bowl, whisk the butter and liquid monk fruit until the mixture is pale and smooth. Mix in the beaten eggs, hazelnuts, and marmalade and whisk again until well incorporated.

4. Add the almond flour, baking soda, baking powder, cinnamon, allspice, anise seed and stir to mix well.

5. Scrape the batter into the prepared baking pan. Bake for 20 minutes, or until the top of the cake springs back when gently pressed with your fingers.

6. Transfer to a wire rack and let the cake cool to room temperature. Serve immediately.

Chapter 8 Fast and Easy Everyday Favorites

Air Fried Broccoli

Prep time: 5 minutes | Cook time: 6 minutes | Serves 1

- 4 egg yolks
- ¼ cup butter, melted
- 2 cups coconut flower
- Salt and pepper, to taste
- 2 cups broccoli florets

1. Preheat the air fryer to 400°F (204°C).
2. In a bowl, whisk the egg yolks and melted butter together. Throw in the coconut flour, salt and pepper, then stir again to combine well.
3. Dip each broccoli floret into the mixture and place in the air fryer basket. Air fry for 6 minutes in batches if necessary. Take care when removing them from the air fryer and serve immediately.

Carrot and Celery Croquettes

Prep time: 10 minutes | Cook time: 6 minutes | Serves 4

- 2 medium-sized carrots, trimmed and grated
- 2 medium-sized celery stalks, trimmed and grated
- ½ cup finely chopped leek
- 1 tablespoon garlic paste
- ¼ teaspoon freshly cracked black pepper
- 1 teaspoon fine sea salt
- 1 tablespoon finely chopped fresh dill
- 1 egg, lightly whisked
- ¼ cup flour
- ¼ teaspoon baking powder
- ½ cup bread crumbs
- Cooking spray
- Chive mayo, for serving

1. Preheat the air fryer to 360°F (182°C).
2. Drain any excess liquid from the carrots and celery by placing them on a paper towel.
3. Stir together the vegetables with all of the other ingredients, save for the bread crumbs and chive mayo.
4. Use your hands to mold 1 tablespoon of the vegetable mixture into a ball and repeat until all of the mixture has been used up. Press down on each ball with your hand or a palette knife. Cover completely with bread crumbs. Spritz the croquettes with cooking spray.
5. Arrange the croquettes in a single layer in the air fryer basket and air fry for 6 minutes.
6. Serve warm with the chive mayo on the side.

Cheesy Potato Patties

Prep time: 5 minutes | Cook time: 10 minutes | Serves 8

- 2 pounds (907 g) white potatoes
- ½ cup finely chopped scallions
- ½ teaspoon freshly ground black pepper, or more to taste
- 1 tablespoon fine sea salt
- ½ teaspoon hot paprika
- 2 cups shredded Colby cheese
- ¼ cup canola oil
- 1 cup crushed crackers

1. Preheat the air fryer to 360°F (182°C).

2. Boil the potatoes until soft. Dry them off and peel them before mashing thoroughly, leaving no lumps.

3. Combine the mashed potatoes with scallions, pepper, salt, paprika, and cheese.

4. Mold the mixture into balls with your hands and press with your palm to flatten them into patties.

5. In a shallow dish, combine the canola oil and crushed crackers. Coat the patties in the crumb mixture.

6. Bake the patties for about 10 minutes, in multiple batches if necessary.

7. Serve hot.

Simple and Easy Croutons

Prep time: 5 minutes | Cook time: 8 minutes | Serves 4

- 2 slices friendly bread
- 1 tablespoon olive oil
- Hot soup, for serving

1. Preheat the air fryer to 390°F (199°C).

2. Cut the slices of bread into medium-size chunks.

3. Brush the air fryer basket with the oil.

4. Place the chunks inside and air fry for at least 8 minutes.

5. Serve with hot soup.

Sweet Corn and Carrot Fritters

Prep time: 10 minutes | Cook time: 8 to 11 minutes | Serves 4

- 1 medium-sized carrot, grated
- 1 yellow onion, finely chopped
- 4 ounces (113 g) canned sweet corn kernels, drained
- 1 teaspoon sea salt flakes
- 1 tablespoon chopped fresh cilantro
- 1 medium-sized egg, whisked
- 2 tablespoons plain milk
- 1 cup grated Parmesan cheese
- ¼ cup flour
- ⅓ teaspoon baking powder
- ⅓ teaspoon sugar
- Cooking spray

1. Preheat the air fryer to 350°F (177°C).

2. Place the grated carrot in a colander and press down to squeeze out any excess moisture. Dry it with a paper towel.

3. Combine the carrots with the remaining ingredients.

4. Mold 1 tablespoon of the mixture into a ball and press it down with your hand or a spoon to flatten it. Repeat until the rest of the mixture is used up.

5. Spritz the balls with cooking spray.

6. Arrange in the air fryer basket, taking care not to overlap any balls. Bake for 8 to 11 minutes, or until they're firm.

7. Serve warm.

Bistro Potato Wedges

Prep time: 10 minutes | Cook time: 13 minutes | Serves 4

- 1 pound (454 g) fingerling potatoes, cut into wedges
- 1 teaspoon extra-virgin olive oil
- ½ teaspoon garlic powder
- Salt and pepper, to taste
- ½ cup raw cashews, soaked in water overnight
- ½ teaspoon ground
- turmeric
- ½ teaspoon paprika
- 1 tablespoon nutritional yeast
- 1 teaspoon fresh lemon juice
- 2 tablespoons to ¼ cup water

1. Preheat the air fryer to 400°F (204°C).

2. In a bowl, toss together the potato wedges, olive oil, garlic powder, and salt and pepper, making sure to coat the potatoes well.

3. Transfer the potatoes to the air fryer basket and air fry for 10 minutes.

4. In the meantime, prepare the cheese sauce. Pulse the cashews, turmeric, paprika, nutritional yeast, lemon juice, and water together in a food processor. Add more water to achieve your desired consistency.

5. When the potatoes are finished cooking, transfer to a bowl and add the cheese sauce on top. Air fry for an additional 3 minutes.

6. Serve hot.

Spinach and Carrot Balls

Prep time: 10 minutes | Cook time: 10 minutes | Serves 4

- 2 slices toasted bread
- 1 carrot, peeled and grated
- 1 package fresh spinach, blanched and chopped
- ½ onion, chopped
- 1 egg, beaten
- ½ teaspoon garlic powder
- 1 teaspoon minced garlic
- 1 teaspoon salt
- ½ teaspoon black pepper
- 1 tablespoon nutritional yeast
- 1 tablespoon flour

1. Preheat the air fryer to 390°F (199°C).

2. In a food processor, pulse the toasted bread to form bread crumbs. Transfer into a shallow dish or bowl.

3. In a bowl, mix together all the other ingredients.

4. Use your hands to shape the mixture into small-sized balls. Roll the balls in the bread crumbs, ensuring to cover them well.

5. Put in the air fryer basket and air fry for 10 minutes.

6. Serve immediately.

Simple Pea Delight

Prep time: 5 minutes | Cook time: 15 minutes | Serves 2 to 4

- 1 cup flour
- 1 teaspoon baking powder
- 3 eggs
- 1 cup coconut milk
- 1 cup cream cheese
- 3 tablespoons pea protein
- ½ cup chicken or turkey strips
- Pinch of sea salt
- 1 cup Mozzarella cheese

1. Preheat the air fryer to 390°F (199°C).
2. In a large bowl, mix all ingredients together using a large wooden spoon.
3. Spoon equal amounts of the mixture into muffin cups and bake for 15 minutes.
4. Serve immediately.

Cheesy Sausage Balls

Prep time: 5 minutes | Cook time: 15 minutes | Serves 6

- 12 ounces (340 g) Jimmy Dean's Sausage
- 6 ounces (170 g) shredded
- Cheddar cheese
- 10 Cheddar cubes

1. Preheat the air fryer to 375°F (191°C).
2. Mix the shredded cheese and sausage.
3. Divide the mixture into 12 equal parts to be stuffed.
4. Add a cube of cheese to the center of the sausage and roll into balls.
5. Air fry for 15 minutes, or until crisp.
6. Serve immediately.

Bacon-Wrapped Beef Hot Dog

Prep time: 5 minutes | Cook time: 10 minutes | Serves 4

- 4 slices sugar-free bacon
- 4 beef hot dogs

1. Preheat the air fryer to 370°F (188°C).
2. Take a slice of bacon and wrap it around the hot dog, securing it with a toothpick. Repeat with the other pieces of bacon and hot dogs, placing each wrapped dog in the air fryer basket.
3. Bake for 10 minutes, turning halfway through.
4. Once hot and crispy, the hot dogs are ready to serve.

Beef Bratwursts

Prep time: 5 minutes | Cook time: 15 minutes | Serves 4

- 4 (3-ounce / 85-g) beef bratwursts

1. Preheat the air fryer to 375°F (191°C).
2. Place the beef bratwursts in the air fryer basket and air fry for 15 minutes, turning once halfway through.

3. Serve hot.

Easy Roasted Asparagus

Prep time: 5 minutes | Cook time: 6 minutes | Serves 4

- 1 pound (454 g) asparagus, trimmed and halved crosswise
- 1 teaspoon extra-virgin
- olive oil
- Salt and pepper, to taste
- Lemon wedges, for serving

1. Preheat the air fryer to 400°F (204°C).
2. Toss the asparagus with the oil, ⅛ teaspoon salt, and ⅛ teaspoon pepper in bowl. Transfer to air fryer basket.
3. Place the basket in air fryer and roast for 6 to 8 minutes, or until tender and bright green, tossing halfway through cooking.
4. Season with salt and pepper and serve with lemon wedges.

Baked Chorizo Scotch Eggs

Prep time: 5 minutes | Cook time: 15 to 20 minutes | Makes 4 eggs

- 1 pound (454 g) Mexican chorizo or other seasoned sausage meat
- 4 soft-boiled eggs plus 1 raw egg
- 1 tablespoon water
- ½ cup all-purpose flour
- 1 cup panko bread crumbs
- Cooking spray

1. Divide the chorizo into 4 equal portions. Flatten each portion into a disc. Place a soft-boiled egg in the center of each disc. Wrap the chorizo around the egg, encasing it completely. Place the encased eggs on a plate and chill for at least 30 minutes.
2. Preheat the air fryer to 360°F (182°C).
3. Beat the raw egg with 1 tablespoon of water. Place the flour on a small plate and the panko on a second plate. Working with 1 egg at a time, roll the encased egg in the flour, then dip it in the egg mixture. Dredge the egg in the panko and place on a plate. Repeat with the remaining eggs.
4. Spray the eggs with oil and place in the air fryer basket. Bake for 10 minutes. Turn and bake for an additional 5 to 10 minutes, or until browned and crisp on all sides.
5. Serve immediately.

Rosemary and Orange Roasted Chickpeas

Prep time: 5 minutes | Cook time: 10 to 12 minutes | Makes 4 cups

- 4 cups cooked chickpeas
- 2 tablespoons vegetable oil
- 1 teaspoon kosher salt
- 1 teaspoon cumin
- 1 teaspoon paprika
- Zest of 1 orange
- 1 tablespoon chopped fresh rosemary

1. Preheat the air fryer to 400°F (204°C).

2. Make sure the chickpeas are completely dry prior to roasting. In a medium bowl, toss the chickpeas with oil, salt, cumin, and paprika.

3. Working in batches, spread the chickpeas in a single layer in the air fryer basket. Air fry for 10 to 12 minutes until crisp, shaking once halfway through.

4. Return the warm chickpeas to the bowl and toss with the orange zest and rosemary. Allow to cool completely.

5. Serve.

Pomegranate Avocado Fries

Prep time: 5 minutes | Cook time: 7 to 8 minutes | Serves 4

- 1 cup panko bread crumbs
- 1 teaspoon kosher salt, plus more for sprinkling
- 1 teaspoon garlic powder
- ½ teaspoon cayenne pepper
- 2 ripe but firm avocados
- 1 egg, beaten with 1 tablespoon water
- Cooking spray
- Pomegranate molasses, for serving

1. Preheat the air fryer to 375°F (191°C).

2. Whisk together the panko, salt, and spices on a plate. Cut each avocado in half and remove the pit. Cut each avocado half into 4 slices and scoop the slices out with a large spoon, taking care to keep the slices intact.

3. Dip each avocado slice in the egg wash and then dredge it in the panko. Place the breaded avocado slices on a plate.

4. Working in 2 batches, arrange half of the avocado slices in a single layer in the air fryer basket. Spray lightly with oil. Bake the slices for 7 to 8 minutes, turning once halfway through. Remove the cooked slices to a platter and repeat with the remaining avocado slices.

5. Sprinkle the warm avocado slices with salt and drizzle with pomegranate molasses. Serve immediately.

Crunchy Fried Okra

Prep time: 5 minutes | Cook time: 8 to 10 minutes | Serves 4

- 1 cup self-rising yellow cornmeal
- 1 teaspoon Italian-style seasoning
- 1 teaspoon paprika
- 1 teaspoon salt
- ½ teaspoon freshly ground black pepper
- 2 large eggs, beaten
- 2 cups okra slices
- Cooking spray

1. Preheat the air fryer to 400°F (204°C). Line the air fryer basket with parchment paper.

2. In a shallow bowl, whisk the cornmeal, Italian-style seasoning, paprika, salt, and pepper until blended. Place the beaten eggs in a second shallow bowl.

3. Add the okra to the beaten egg and stir to coat. Add the

egg and okra mixture to the cornmeal mixture and stir until coated.

4. Place the okra on the parchment and spritz it with oil.

5. Air fry for 4 minutes. Shake the basket, spritz the okra with oil, and air fry for 4 to 6 minutes more until lightly browned and crispy.

6. Serve immediately.

Buttery Sweet Potatoes

Prep time: 5 minutes | Cook time: 10 minutes | Serves 4

- 2 tablespoons butter, melted
- 1 tablespoon light brown sugar
- 2 sweet potatoes, peeled and cut into ½-inch cubes
- Cooking spray

1. Preheat the air fryer to 400°F (204°C). Line the air fryer basket with parchment paper.

2. In a medium bowl, stir together the melted butter and brown sugar until blended. Toss the sweet potatoes in the butter mixture until coated.

3. Place the sweet potatoes on the parchment and spritz with oil.

4. Air fry for 5 minutes. Shake the basket, spritz the sweet potatoes with oil, and air fry for 5 minutes more until they're soft enough to cut with a fork.

5. Serve immediately.

Corn Fritters

Prep time: 15 minutes | Cook time: 8 minutes | Serves 6

- 1 cup self-rising flour
- 1 tablespoon sugar
- 1 teaspoon salt
- 1 large egg, lightly beaten
- ¼ cup buttermilk
- ¾ cup corn kernels
- ¼ cup minced onion
- Cooking spray

1. Preheat the air fryer to 350°F (177°C). Line the air fryer basket with parchment paper.

2. In a medium bowl, whisk the flour, sugar, and salt until blended. Stir in the egg and buttermilk. Add the corn and minced onion. Mix well. Shape the corn fritter batter into 12 balls.

3. Place the fritters on the parchment and spritz with oil. Bake for 4 minutes. Flip the fritters, spritz them with oil, and bake for 4 minutes more until firm and lightly browned.

4. Serve immediately.

Bacon and Green Beans

Prep time: 15 minutes | Cook time: 8 to 10 minutes | Serves 4

- 2 (14.5-ounce / 411-g) cans cut green beans, drained
- 4 bacon slices, air-fried and diced

- ¼ cup minced onion
- 1 tablespoon distilled white vinegar
- 1 teaspoon freshly squeezed lemon juice
- ½ teaspoon salt
- ½ teaspoon freshly ground black pepper
- Cooking spray

1. Preheat the air fryer to 370°F (188°C).
2. Spritz a baking pan with oil. In the prepared pan, stir together the green beans, bacon, onion, vinegar, lemon juice, salt, and pepper until blended.
3. Place the pan on the air fryer basket.
4. Air fry for 4 minutes. Stir the green beans and air fry for 4 to 6 minutes more until soft.
5. Serve immediately.

Frico

Prep time: 5 minutes | Cook time: 5 minutes | Serves 2

- 1 cup shredded aged Manchego cheese
- 1 teaspoon all-purpose flour
- ½ teaspoon cumin seeds
- ¼ teaspoon cracked black pepper

1. Preheat the air fryer to 375°F (191°C). Line the air fryer basket with parchment paper.
2. Combine the cheese and flour in a bowl. Stir to mix well. Spread the mixture in the basket into a 4-inch round.
3. Combine the cumin and black pepper in a small bowl. Stir to mix well. Sprinkle the cumin mixture over the cheese round.
4. Air fry 5 minutes or until the cheese is lightly browned and frothy.
5. Use tongs to transfer the cheese wafer onto a plate and slice to serve.

Garlicky Baked Cherry Tomatoes

Prep time: 5 minutes | Cook time: 4 to 6 minutes | Serves 2

- 2 cups cherry tomatoes
- 1 clove garlic, thinly sliced
- 1 teaspoon olive oil
- ⅛ teaspoon kosher salt
- 1 tablespoon freshly chopped basil, for topping
- Cooking spray

1. Preheat the air fryer to 360°F (182°C). Spritz the air fryer baking pan with cooking spray and set aside.
2. In a large bowl, toss together the cherry tomatoes, sliced garlic, olive oil, and kosher salt. Spread the mixture in an even layer in the prepared pan.
3. Bake in the preheated air fryer for 4 to 6 minutes, or until the tomatoes become soft and wilted.
4. Transfer to a bowl and rest for 5 minutes. Top with the chopped basil and serve warm.

Garlicky Knots with Parsley

Prep time: 10 minutes | Cook time: 10 minutes | Makes 8 knots

- 1 teaspoon dried parsley
- ¼ cup melted butter
- 2 teaspoons garlic powder
- 1 (11-ounce / 312-g) tube refrigerated French bread dough, cut into 8 slices

1. Preheat the air fryer to 350°F (177°C).
2. Combine the parsley, butter, and garlic powder in a bowl. Stir to mix well.
3. Place the French bread dough slices on a clean work surface, then roll each slice into a 6-inch long rope. Tie the ropes into knots and arrange them on a plate. Brush the knots with butter mixture.
4. Transfer the knots into the air fryer. You need to work in batches to avoid overcrowding.
5. Air fry for 5 minutes or until the knots are golden brown. Flip the knots halfway through the cooking time.
6. Serve immediately.

Garlicky Zoodles

Prep time: 10 minutes | Cook time: 10 minutes | Serves 4

- 2 large zucchini, peeled and spiralized
- 2 large yellow summer squash, peeled and spiralized
- 1 tablespoon olive oil, divided
- ½ teaspoon kosher salt
- 1 garlic clove, whole
- 2 tablespoons fresh basil, chopped
- Cooking spray

1. Preheat the air fryer to 360°F (182°C). Spritz the air fryer basket with cooking spray.
2. Combine the zucchini and summer squash with 1 teaspoon olive oil and salt in a large bowl. Toss to coat well.
3. Transfer the zucchini and summer squash in the preheated air fryer and add the garlic.
4. Air fry for 10 minutes or until tender and fragrant. Toss the spiralized zucchini and summer squash halfway through the cooking time.
5. Transfer the cooked zucchini and summer squash onto a plate and set aside.
6. Remove the garlic from the air fryer and allow to cool for a few minutes. Mince the garlic and combine with remaining olive oil in a small bowl. Stir to mix well.
7. Drizzle the spiralized zucchini and summer squash with garlic oil and sprinkle with basil. Toss to serve.

Chapter 9 Holiday Specials

Garlicky Olive Stromboli

Prep time: 25 minutes | Cook time: 25 minutes | Serves 8

- 4 large cloves garlic, unpeeled
- 3 tablespoons grated Parmesan cheese
- ½ cup packed fresh basil leaves
- ½ cup marinated, pitted green and black olives
- ¼ teaspoon crushed red

- pepper
- ½ pound (227 g) pizza dough, at room temperature
- 4 ounces (113 g) sliced provolone cheese (about 8 slices)
- Cooking spray

1. Preheat the air fryer to 370°F (188°C). Spritz the air fryer basket with cooking spray.

2. Put the unpeeled garlic in the air fryer basket.

3. Air fry for 10 minutes or until the garlic is softened completely. Remove them from the air fryer and allow to cool until you can handle.

4. Peel the garlic and place into a food processor with 2 tablespoons of Parmesan, basil, olives, and crushed red pepper. Pulse to mix well. Set aside.

5. Arrange the pizza dough on a clean work surface, then roll it out with a rolling pin into a rectangle. Cut the rectangle in half.

6. Sprinkle half of the garlic mixture over each rectangle half, and leave ½-inch edges uncover. Top them with the provolone cheese.

7. Brush one long side of each rectangle half with water, then roll them up. Spritz the air fryer basket with cooking spray. Transfer the rolls in the preheated air fryer. Spritz with cooking spray and scatter with remaining Parmesan.

8. Air fry the rolls for 15 minutes or until golden brown. Flip the rolls halfway through.

9. Remove the rolls from the air fryer and allow to cool for a few minutes before serving.

Golden Nuggets

Prep time: 15 minutes | Cook time: 4 minutes per batch | Makes 20 nuggets

- 1 cup all-purpose flour, plus more for dusting
- 1 teaspoon baking powder
- ½ teaspoon butter, at room temperature, plus more for brushing
- ¼ teaspoon salt

- ¼ cup water
- ⅛ teaspoon onion powder
- ¼ teaspoon garlic powder
- ⅛ teaspoon seasoning salt
- Cooking spray

1. Preheat the air fryer to 370°F (188°C). Line the air fryer basket with parchment paper.

2. Mix the flour, baking powder, butter, and salt in a large bowl. Stir to mix well. Gradually whisk in the water until a sanity dough forms.

3. Put the dough on a lightly floured work surface, then roll it out into a ½-inch thick rectangle with a rolling pin.

4. Cut the dough into about twenty 1- or 2-inch squares, then arrange the squares in a single layer in the preheated air fryer. Spritz with cooking spray. You need to work in batches to avoid overcrowding.

5. Combine onion powder, garlic powder, and seasoning salt in a small bowl. Stir to mix well, then sprinkle the squares with the powder mixture.

6. Air fry the dough squares for 4 minutes or until golden brown. Flip the squares halfway through the cooking time.

7. Remove the golden nuggets from the air fryer and brush with more butter immediately. Serve warm.

Jewish Blintzes

Prep time: 5 minutes | Cook time: 10 minutes | Makes 8 blintzes

- 2 (7½-ounce / 213-g) packages farmer cheese, mashed
- ¼ cup cream cheese
- ¼ teaspoon vanilla extract
- ¼ cup granulated white sugar
- 8 egg roll wrappers
- 4 tablespoons butter, melted

1. Preheat the air fryer to 375°F (191°C).

2. Combine the farmer cheese, cream cheese, vanilla extract, and sugar in a bowl. Stir to mix well.

3. Unfold the egg roll wrappers on a clean work surface, spread ¼ cup of the filling at the edge of each wrapper and leave a ½-inch edge uncovering.

4. Wet the edges of the wrappers with water and fold the uncovered edge over the filling. Fold the left and right sides in the center, then tuck the edge under the filling and fold to wrap the filling.

5. Brush the wrappers with melted butter, then arrange the wrappers in a single layer in the preheated air fryer, seam side down. Leave a little space between each two wrappers. Work in batches to avoid overcrowding.

6. Air fry for 10 minutes or until golden brown.

7. Serve immediately.

Milky Pecan Tart

Prep time: 2hours 25 minutes | Cook time: 30 minutes | Serves 8

Tart Crust:
- ¼ cup firmly packed brown sugar
- ⅓ cup butter, softened
- 1 cup all-purpose flour
- ¼ teaspoon kosher salt

Filling:
- ¼ cup whole milk
- 4 tablespoons butter, diced
- ½ cup packed brown sugar
- ¼ cup pure maple syrup
- 1½ cups finely chopped pecans
- ¼ teaspoon pure vanilla extract

- ¼ teaspoon sea salt

1. Preheat the air fryer to 350°F (177°C). Line a baking pan with aluminum foil, then spritz the pan with cooking spray.

2. Stir the brown sugar and butter in a bowl with a hand mixer until puffed, then add the flour and salt and stir until crumbled.

3. Pour the mixture in the prepared baking pan and tilt the pan to coat the bottom evenly.

4. Arrange the pan in the preheated air fryer. Bake for 13 minutes or until the crust is golden brown.

5. Meanwhile, pour the milk, butter, sugar, and maple syrup in a saucepan. Stir to mix well. Bring to a simmer, then cook for 1 more minute. Stir constantly.

6. Turn off the heat and mix the pecans and vanilla into the filling mixture.

7. Pour the filling mixture over the golden crust and spread with a spatula to coat the crust evenly.

8. Bake in the air fryer for an additional 12 minutes or until the filling mixture is set and frothy.

9. Remove the baking pan from the air fryer and sprinkle with salt. Allow to sit for 10 minutes or until cooled.

10. Transfer the pan to the refrigerator to chill for at least 2 hours, then remove the aluminum foil and slice to serve.

Pigs in a Blanket

Prep time: 10 minutes | Cook time: 8 minutes per batch | Makes 16 rolls

- 1 can refrigerated crescent roll dough
- 1 small package mini smoked sausages, patted dry
- 2 tablespoons melted butter
- 2 teaspoons sesame seeds
- 1 teaspoon onion powder

1. Preheat the air fryer to 330°F (166°C).

2. Place the crescent roll dough on a clean work surface and separate into 8 pieces. Cut each piece in half and you will have 16 triangles.

3. Make the pigs in the blanket: Arrange each sausage on each dough triangle, then roll the sausages up.

4. Brush the pigs with melted butter and place half of the pigs in the blanket in the preheated air fryer. Sprinkle with sesame seeds and onion powder.

5. Bake for 8 minutes or until the pigs are fluffy and golden brown. Flip the pigs halfway through.

6. Serve immediately.

Breaded Dill Pickles with Buttermilk Dressing

Prep time: 45 minutes | Cook time: 8 minutes | Serves 6 to 8

Buttermilk Dressing:

- ¼ cup buttermilk
- ¼ cup chopped scallions
- ¾ cup mayonnaise
- ½ cup sour cream
- ½ teaspoon cayenne pepper
- ½ teaspoon onion powder
- ½ teaspoon garlic powder
- 1 tablespoon chopped chives
- 2 tablespoons chopped fresh dill
- Kosher salt and ground
- black pepper, to taste

Fried Dill Pickles:

- ¾ cup all-purpose flour
- 1 (2-pound / 907-g) jar kosher dill pickles, cut into 4 spears, drained
- 2½ cups panko bread crumbs
- 2 eggs, beaten with 2 tablespoons water
- Kosher salt and ground black pepper, to taste
- Cooking spray

1. Combine the ingredients for the dressing in a bowl. Stir to mix well.
2. Wrap the bowl in plastic and refrigerate for 30 minutes or until ready to serve.
3. Pour the flour in a bowl and sprinkle with salt and ground black pepper. Stir to mix well. Put the bread crumbs in a separate bowl. Pour the beaten eggs in a third bowl.
4. Dredge the pickle spears in the flour, then into the eggs, and then into the panko to coat well. Shake the excess off.
5. Arrange the pickle spears in a single layer in the air fry basket and spritz with cooking spray.
6. Place the basket on the air fry position.
7. Select Air Fry, set temperature to 400°F (205°C) and set time to 8 minutes. Flip the pickle spears halfway through the cooking time.
8. When cooking is complete, remove the pan from the air fryer grill.
9. Serve the pickle spears with buttermilk dressing.

Risotto Croquettes with Tomato Sauce

Prep time: 1 hour 40 minutes | Cook time: 54 minutes | Serves 6

Risotto Croquettes:

- 4 tablespoons unsalted butter
- 1 small yellow onion, minced
- 1 cup Arborio rice
- 3½ cups chicken stock
- ½ cup dry white wine
- 3 eggs
- Zest of 1 lemon
- ½ cup grated Parmesan

cheese

- 2 ounces (57 g) fresh Mozzarella cheese
- ¼ cup peas
- 2 tablespoons water
- ½ cup all-purpose flour
- 1½ cups panko bread crumbs
- Kosher salt and ground black pepper, to taste
- Cooking spray

Tomato Sauce:

- 2 tablespoons extra-virgin olive oil
- 4 cloves garlic, minced
- ¼ teaspoon red pepper flakes
- 1 (28-ounce / 794-g) can crushed tomatoes
- 2 teaspoons granulated sugar
- Kosher salt and ground black pepper, to taste

1. Melt the butter in a pot over medium heat, then add the onion and salt to taste. Sauté for 5 minutes or until the onion in translucent.
2. Add the rice and stir to coat well. Cook for 3 minutes or until the rice is lightly browned. Pour in the chicken stock and wine.
3. Bring to a boil. Then cook for 20 minutes or until the rice is tender and liquid is almost absorbed.
4. Make the risotto: When the rice is cooked, break the egg into the pot. Add the lemon zest and Parmesan cheese. Sprinkle with salt and ground black pepper. Stir to mix well.
5. Pour the risotto in a baking sheet, then level with a spatula to spread the risotto evenly. Wrap the baking sheet in plastic and refrigerate for1 hour.
6. Meanwhile, heat the olive oil in a saucepan over medium heat until shimmering.
7. Add the garlic and sprinkle with red pepper flakes. Sauté for a minute or until fragrant.
8. Add the crushed tomatoes and sprinkle with sugar. Stir to mix well. Bring to a boil. Reduce the heat to low and simmer for 15 minutes or until lightly thickened. Sprinkle with salt and pepper to taste. Set aside until ready to serve.
9. Remove the risotto from the refrigerator. Scoop the risotto into twelve 2-inch balls, then flatten the balls with your hands.
10. Arrange a about ½-inch piece of Mozzarella and 5 peas in the center of each flattened ball, then wrap them back into balls.
11. Transfer the balls to a baking sheet lined with parchment paper, then refrigerate for 15 minutes or until firm.
12. Whisk the remaining 2 eggs with 2 tablespoons of water in a bowl. Pour the flour in a second bowl and pour the panko in a third bowl.
13. Dredge the risotto balls in the bowl of flour first, then into the eggs, and then into the panko. Shake the excess off.
14. Transfer the balls to the air fry basket and spritz with cooking spray.
15. Place the basket on the bake position.
16. Select Bake, set temperature to 400°F (205°C) and set time to 10 minutes. Flip the balls halfway through the cooking time.

[73]

17. When cooking is complete, the balls should be until golden brown.

18. Serve the risotto balls with the tomato sauce.

Fast Banana Cake

Prep time: 25 minutes | Cook time: 20 minutes | Serves 8

- 1 cup plus 1 tablespoon all-purpose flour
- ¼ teaspoon baking soda
- ¾ teaspoon baking powder
- ¼ teaspoon salt
- 9½ tablespoons granulated white sugar
- 5 tablespoons butter, at room temperature
- 2½ small ripe bananas, peeled
- 2 large eggs
- 5 tablespoons buttermilk
- 1 teaspoon vanilla extract
- Cooking spray

1. Spritz a baking pan with cooking spray.

2. Combine the flour, baking powder, salt, and baking soda in a large bowl. Stir to mix well.

3. Beat the sugar and butter in a separate bowl with a hand mixer on medium speed for 3 minutes.

4. Beat in the bananas, eggs, vanilla, and buttermilk extract into the sugar and butter mix with a hand mixer.

5. Pour in the flour mixture and whip with hand mixer until sanity and smooth.

6. Scrape the batter into the pan and level the batter with a spatula.

7. Place the pan on the bake position.

8. Select Bake, set temperature to 325°F (163°C) and set time to 20 minutes.

9. After 15 minutes, remove the pan from the air fryer grill. Check the doneness. Return the pan to the air fryer grill and continue cooking.

10. When done, a toothpick inserted in the center should come out clean.

11. Invert the cake on a cooling rack and allow to cool for 15 minutes before slicing to serve.

Classic Mexican Churros

Prep time: 35 minutes | Cook time: 10 minutes | Makes 12 churros

- 4 tablespoons butter
- ¼ teaspoon salt
- ½ cup water
- ½ cup all-purpose flour
- 2 large eggs
- 2 teaspoons ground cinnamon
- ¼ cup granulated white sugar
- Cooking spray

1. Put the butter, salt, and water in a saucepan. Bring to a boil until the butter is melted on high heat. Keep stirring.

2. Reduce the heat to medium and fold in the flour to form a dough. Keep cooking and stirring until the dough is dried out and coat the pan with a crust.

3. Turn off the heat and scrape the dough in a large bowl. Allow to cool for 15 minutes.

4. Break and whisk the eggs into the dough with a hand mixer until the dough is sanity and firm enough to shape.

5. Scoop up 1 tablespoon of the dough and roll it into a ½-inch-diameter and 2-inch-long cylinder. Repeat with remaining dough to make 12 cylinders in total.

6. Combine the sugar and cinnamon in a large bowl and dunk the cylinders into the cinnamon mix to coat.

7. Arrange the cylinders on a plate and refrigerate for 20 minutes.

8. Spritz the air fry basket with cooking spray. Place the cylinders in the air fry basket and spritz with cooking spray.

9. Place the basket on the air fry position.

10. Select Air Fry, set temperature to 375°F (190°C) and set time to 10 minutes. Flip the cylinders halfway through the cooking time.

11. When cooked, the cylinders should be golden brown and fluffy.

12. Serve immediately.

Milk-Butter Pecan Tart

Prep time: 2 hours 25 minutes | Cook time: 26 minutes | Serves 8

Tart Crust:

- ¼ cup firmly packed brown sugar
- ⅓ cup butter, softened
- 1 cup all-purpose flour
- ¼ teaspoon kosher salt

Filling:

- ¼ cup whole milk
- 4 tablespoons butter, diced
- ½ cup packed brown sugar
- ¼ cup pure maple syrup
- 1½ cups finely chopped pecans
- ¼ teaspoon pure vanilla extract
- ¼ teaspoon sea salt

1. Line a baking pan with aluminum foil, then spritz the pan with cooking spray.

2. Stir the brown sugar and butter in a bowl with a hand mixer until puffed, then add the flour and salt and stir until crumbled.

3. Pour the mixture in the prepared baking pan and tilt the pan to coat the bottom evenly.

4. Place the pan on the bake position. Place the pan on the bake position.

5. Select Bake, set temperature to 350°F (180°C) and set time to 13 minutes.

6. When done, the crust will be golden brown.

7. Meanwhile, pour the milk, butter, sugar, and maple syrup in a saucepan. Stir to mix well. Bring to a simmer, then cook for 1 more minute. Stir constantly.

8. Turn off the heat and mix the pecans and vanilla into the filling mixture.

9. Pour the filling mixture over the golden crust and spread with a spatula to coat the crust evenly.

10. Place the pan on the bake position.

11. Select Bake and set time to 12 minutes. When cooked, the filling mixture should be set and frothy.

12. Remove the baking pan from the air fryer grill and sprinkle with salt. Allow to sit for 10 minutes or until cooled.

13. Transfer the pan to the refrigerator to chill for at least 2 hours, then remove the aluminum foil and slice to serve.

Chocolate-Glazed Custard Donut Holes

Prep time: 1 hour 50 minutes | Cook time: 4 minutes | Makes 24 donut holes

Dough:
- 1½ cups bread flour
- 2 egg yolks
- 1 teaspoon active dry yeast
- ½ cup warm milk
- ½ teaspoon pure vanilla extract
- 2 tablespoons butter, melted
- 1 tablespoon sugar
- ¼ teaspoon salt
- Cooking spray

Custard Filling:
- 1 (3.4-ounce / 96-g) box French vanilla instant pudding mix
- ¼ cup heavy cream
- ¾ cup whole milk

Chocolate Glaze:
- ⅓ cup heavy cream
- 1 cup chocolate chips

Special Equipment:
- A pastry bag with a long tip

1. Combine the ingredients for the dough in a food processor, then pulse until a satiny dough ball forms.

2. Transfer the dough on a lightly floured work surface, then knead for 2 minutes by hand and shape the dough back to a ball.

3. Spritz a large bowl with cooking spray, then transfer the dough ball into the bowl. Wrap the bowl in plastic and let it rise for 1½ hours or until it doubled in size.

4. Transfer the risen dough on a floured work surface, then shape it into a 24-inch long log. Cut the log into 24 parts and shape each part into a ball.

5. Transfer the balls on two baking sheets and let sit to rise for 30 more minutes.

6. Spritz the balls with cooking spray.

7. Place the baking sheets on the bake position.

8. Select Bake, set temperature to 400°F (205°C) and set time to 4 minutes. Flip the balls halfway through the cooking time.

9. When cooked, the balls should be golden brown.

10. Meanwhile, combine the ingredients for the filling in a large bowl and whisk for 2 minutes with a hand mixer until well combined.

11. Pour the heavy cream in a saucepan, then bring to a boil. Put the chocolate chips in a small bowl and pour in the boiled heavy cream immediately. Mix until the chocolate chips are melted and the mixture is smooth.

12. Transfer the baked donut holes to a large plate, then pierce a hole into each donut hole and lightly hollow them.

13. Pour the filling in a pastry bag with a long tip and gently squeeze the filling into the donut holes. Then top the donut holes with chocolate glaze.

14. Allow to sit for 10 minutes, then serve.

Sausage Rolls

Prep time: 10 minutes | Cook time: 8 minutes | Makes 16 rolls

- 1 can refrigerated crescent roll dough
- 1 small package mini smoked sausages, patted dry
- 2 tablespoons melted butter
- 2 teaspoons sesame seeds
- 1 teaspoon onion powder

1. Place the crescent roll dough on a clean work surface and separate into 8 pieces. Cut each piece in half and you will have 16 triangles.

2. Make the pigs in the blanket: Arrange each sausage on each dough triangle, then roll the sausages up.

3. Brush the pigs with melted butter and place of the pigs in the blanket in the air fry basket. Sprinkle with sesame seeds and onion powder.

4. Place the basket on the bake position.

5. Select Bake, set temperature to 330°F (166°C) and set time to 8 minutes. Flip the pigs halfway through the cooking time.

6. When cooking is complete, the pigs should be fluffy and golden brown.

7. Serve immediately.

Cream-Glazed Cinnamon Rolls

Prep time: 2 hours 15 minutes | Cook time: 5 minutes | Serves 8

- 1 pound (454 g) frozen bread dough, thawed
- 2 tablespoons melted butter
- 1½ tablespoons cinnamon
- ¾ cup brown sugar
- Cooking spray

Cream Glaze:
- 4 ounces (113 g) softened cream cheese

- ½ teaspoon vanilla extract
- 2 tablespoons melted butter
- 1¼ cups powdered erythritol

1. Place the bread dough on a clean work surface, then roll the dough out into a rectangle with a rolling pin.

2. Brush the top of the dough with melted butter and leave 1-inch edges uncovered.

3. Combine the cinnamon and sugar in a small bowl, then sprinkle the dough with the cinnamon mixture.

4. Roll the dough over tightly, then cut the dough log into 8 portions. Wrap the portions in plastic, better separately, and let sit to rise for 1 or 2 hours.

5. Meanwhile, combine the ingredients for the glaze in a separate small bowl. Stir to mix well.

6. Spritz the perforated pan with cooking spray. Transfer the risen rolls to the perforated pan.

7. Select Air Fry. Set temperature to 350°F (180°C) and set time to 5 minutes. Press Start to begin preheating.

8. Once the oven has preheated, place the pan into the oven. Flip the rolls halfway through the cooking time.

9. When cooking is complete, the rolls will be golden brown.

10. Serve the rolls with the glaze.

Buttermilk Chocolate Cake

Prep time: 20 minutes | Cook time: 20 minutes | Serves 8

- 1 cup all-purpose flour
- ⅔ cup granulated white sugar
- ¼ cup unsweetened cocoa powder
- ¾ teaspoon baking soda
- ¼ teaspoon salt
- ⅔ cup buttermilk
- 2 tablespoons plus 2 teaspoons vegetable oil
- 1 teaspoon vanilla extract
- Cooking spray

1. Spritz a baking pan with cooking spray.

2. Combine the flour, cocoa powder, baking soda, sugar, and salt in a large bowl. Stir to mix well.

3. Mix in the buttermilk, vanilla, and vegetable oil. Keep stirring until it forms a grainy and thick dough.

4. Scrape the chocolate batter from the bowl and transfer to the pan, level the batter in an even layer with a spatula.

5. Select Bake. Set temperature to 325°F (163°C) and set time to 20 minutes. Press Start to begin preheating.

6. Once preheated, place the pan into the oven.

7. After 15 minutes, remove the pan from the oven. Check the doneness. Return the pan to the oven and continue cooking.

8. When done, a toothpick inserted in the center should come out clean.

9. Invert the cake on a cooling rack and allow to cool for 15 minutes before slicing to serve.

Teriyaki-Marinated Shrimp Skewers

Prep time: 10 minutes | Cook time: 6 minutes | Makes 12 skewered shrimp

- 1½ tablespoons mirin
- 1½ teaspoons ginger juice
- 1½ tablespoons soy sauce
- 12 large shrimp (about 20 shrimps per pound) peeled and deveined
- 1 large egg
- ¾ cup panko bread crumbs
- Cooking spray

1. Combine the mirin, ginger juice, and soy sauce in a large bowl. Stir to mix well.

2. Dunk the shrimp in the bowl of mirin mixture, then wrap the bowl in plastic and refrigerate for 1 hour to marinate.

3. Spritz the perforated pan with cooking spray.

4. Run twelve 4-inch skewers through each shrimp.

5. Whisk the egg in the bowl of marinade to combine well. Pour the bread crumbs on a plate.

6. Dredge the shrimp skewers in the egg mixture, then shake the excess off and roll over the bread crumbs to coat well.

7. Arrange the shrimp skewers in the perforated pan and spritz with cooking spray.

8. Select Air Fry. Set temperature to 400°F (205°C) and set time to 6 minutes. Press Start to begin preheating.

9. Once preheated, place the pan into the oven. Flip the shrimp skewers halfway through the cooking time.

10. When done, the shrimp will be opaque and firm.

11. Serve immediately.

Garlic Nuggets

Prep time: 15 minutes | Cook time: 4 minutes | Makes 20 nuggets

- 1 cup all-purpose flour, plus more for dusting
- 1 teaspoon baking powder
- ½ teaspoon butter, at room temperature, plus more for brushing
- ¼ teaspoon salt
- ¼ cup water
- ⅛ teaspoon onion powder
- ¼ teaspoon garlic powder
- ⅛ teaspoon seasoning salt
- Cooking spray

1. Line the perforated pan with parchment paper.

2. Mix the flour, baking powder, butter, and salt in a large bowl. Stir to mix well. Gradually whisk in the water until a sanity dough forms.

3. Put the dough on a lightly floured work surface, then roll it

out into a ½-inch thick rectangle with a rolling pin.

4. Cut the dough into about twenty 1- or 2-inch squares, then arrange the squares in a single layer in the perforated pan. Spritz with cooking spray.

5. Combine onion powder, garlic powder, and seasoning salt in a small bowl. Stir to mix well, then sprinkle the squares with the powder mixture.

6. Select Air Fry. Set temperature to 370°F (188°C) and set time to 4 minutes. Press Start to begin preheating.

7. Once the oven has preheated, place the pan into the oven. Flip the squares halfway through the cooking time.

8. When cooked, the dough squares should be golden brown.

9. Remove the golden nuggets from the oven and brush with more butter immediately. Serve warm.

Vanilla Cheese Blintzes

Prep time: 5 minutes | Cook time: 10 minutes | Makes 8 blintzes

- 2 (7½-ounce / 213-g) packages farmer cheese, mashed
- ¼ cup cream cheese
- ¼ teaspoon vanilla extract
- ¼ cup granulated white sugar
- 8 egg roll wrappers
- 4 tablespoons butter, melted

1. Combine the farmer cheese, cream cheese, vanilla extract, and sugar in a bowl. Stir to mix well.

2. Unfold the egg roll wrappers on a clean work surface, spread ¼ cup of the filling at the edge of each wrapper and leave a ½-inch edge uncovering.

3. Wet the edges of the wrappers with water and fold the uncovered edge over the filling. Fold the left and right sides in the center, then tuck the edge under the filling and fold to wrap the filling.

4. Brush the wrappers with melted butter, then arrange the wrappers in a single layer in the perforated pan, seam side down. Leave a little space between each two wrappers.

5. Select Air Fry. Set temperature to 375°F (190°C) and set time to 10 minutes. Press Start to begin preheating.

6. Once preheated, place the pan into the oven.

7. When cooking is complete, the wrappers will be golden brown.

8. Serve immediately.

Maple Pecan Tart

Prep time: 2 hours 25 minutes | Cook time: 26 minutes | Serves 8

Tart Crust:

- ¼ cup firmly packed brown sugar
- ⅓ cup butter, softened
- 1 cup all-purpose flour
- ¼ teaspoon kosher salt

Filling:

- ¼ cup whole milk
- 4 tablespoons butter, diced
- ½ cup packed brown sugar
- ¼ cup pure maple syrup
- 1½ cups finely chopped pecans
- ¼ teaspoon pure vanilla extract
- ¼ teaspoon sea salt

1. Line a baking pan with aluminum foil, then spritz the pan with cooking spray.

2. Stir the brown sugar and butter in a bowl with a hand mixer until puffed, then add the flour and salt and stir until crumbled.

3. Pour the mixture in the prepared baking pan and tilt the pan to coat the bottom evenly.

4. Select Bake. Set temperature to 350°F (180°C) and set time to 13 minutes. Press Start to begin preheating.

5. Once the oven has preheated, place the pan into the oven.

6. When done, the crust will be golden brown.

7. Meanwhile, pour the milk, butter, sugar, and maple syrup in a saucepan. Stir to mix well. Bring to a simmer, then cook for 1 more minute. Stir constantly.

8. Turn off the heat and mix the pecans and vanilla into the filling mixture.

9. Pour the filling mixture over the golden crust and spread with a spatula to coat the crust evenly.

10. Select Bake and set time to 12 minutes. Place the pan into the oven. When cooked, the filling mixture should be set and frothy.

11. Remove the baking pan from the oven and sprinkle with salt. Allow to sit for 10 minutes or until cooled.

12. Transfer the pan to the refrigerator to chill for at least 2 hours, then remove the aluminum foil and slice to serve.

Asiago Balls

Prep time: 37 minutes | Cook time: 12 minutes | Makes 12 balls

- 2 tablespoons butter, plus more for greasing
- ½ cup milk
- 1½ cups tapioca flour
- ½ teaspoon salt
- 1 large egg
- ⅔ cup finely grated aged Asiago cheese

1. Put the butter in a saucepan and pour in the milk, heat over medium heat until the liquid boils. Keep stirring.

2. Turn off the heat and mix in the tapioca flour and salt to form a soft dough. Transfer the dough in a large bowl, then wrap the bowl in plastic and let sit for 15 minutes.

3. Break the egg in the bowl of dough and whisk with a hand mixer for 2 minutes or until a sanity dough forms. Fold the cheese in the dough. Cover the bowl in plastic again and let sit for 10 more minutes.

4. Grease a baking pan with butter.

5. Scoop 2 tablespoons of the dough into the baking pan. Repeat with the remaining dough to make dough 12 balls. Keep a little distance between each two balls.

6. Select Bake. Set temperature to 375°F (190°C) and set time to 12 minutes. Press Start to begin preheating.

7. Once preheated, place the pan into the oven. Flip the balls halfway through the cooking time.

8. When cooking is complete, the balls should be golden brown and fluffy.

9. Remove the balls from the oven and allow to cool for 5 minutes before serving.

Sriracha Shrimp with Mayo

Prep time: 15 minutes | Cook time: 10 minutes | Serves 4

- 1 tablespoon Sriracha sauce
- 1 teaspoon Worcestershire sauce
- 2 tablespoons sweet chili sauce
- ¾ cup mayonnaise
- 1 egg, beaten
- 1 cup panko bread crumbs
- 1 pound (454 g) raw shrimp, shelled and deveined, rinsed and drained
- Lime wedges, for serving
- Cooking spray

1. Spritz the perforated pan with cooking spray.

2. Combine the Sriracha sauce, Worcestershire sauce, chili sauce, and mayo in a bowl. Stir to mix well. Reserve ⅓ cup of the mixture as the dipping sauce.

3. Combine the remaining sauce mixture with the beaten egg. Stir to mix well. Put the panko in a separate bowl.

4. Dredge the shrimp in the sauce mixture first, then into the panko. Roll the shrimp to coat well. Shake the excess off.

5. Place the shrimp in the perforated pan, then spritz with cooking spray.

6. Select Air Fry. Set temperature to 360°F (182°C) and set time to 10 minutes. Press Start to begin preheating.

7. Once preheated, place the pan into the oven. Flip the shrimp halfway through the cooking time.

8. When cooking is complete, the shrimp should be opaque.

9. Remove the shrimp from the oven and serve with reserve sauce mixture and squeeze the lime wedges over.

Appendix 1 Measurement Conversion Chart

VOLUME EQUIVALENTS(DRY)

US STANDARD	METRIC (APPROXIMATE)
1/8 teaspoon	0.5 mL
1/4 teaspoon	1 mL
1/2 teaspoon	2 mL
3/4 teaspoon	4 mL
1 teaspoon	5 mL
1 tablespoon	15 mL
1/4 cup	59 mL
1/2 cup	118 mL
3/4 cup	177 mL
1 cup	235 mL
2 cups	475 mL
3 cups	700 mL
4 cups	1 L

VOLUME EQUIVALENTS(LIQUID)

US STANDARD	US STANDARD (OUNCES)	METRIC (APPROXIMATE)
2 tablespoons	1 fl.oz.	30 mL
1/4 cup	2 fl.oz.	60 mL
1/2 cup	4 fl.oz.	120 mL
1 cup	8 fl.oz.	240 mL
1 1/2 cup	12 fl.oz.	355 mL
2 cups or 1 pint	16 fl.oz.	475 mL
4 cups or 1 quart	32 fl.oz.	1 L
1 gallon	128 fl.oz.	4 L

TEMPERATURES EQUIVALENTS

FAHRENHEIT(F)	CELSIUS(C) (APPROXIMATE)
225 °F	107 °C
250 °F	120 °C
275 °F	135 °C
300 °F	150 °C
325 °F	160 °C
350 °F	180 °C
375 °F	190 °C
400 °F	205 °C
425 °F	220 °C
450 °F	235 °C
475 °F	245 °C
500 °F	260 °C

WEIGHT EQUIVALENTS

US STANDARD	METRIC (APPROXIMATE)
1 ounce	28 g
2 ounces	57 g
5 ounces	142 g
10 ounces	284 g
15 ounces	425 g
16 ounces (1 pound)	455 g
1.5 pounds	680 g
2 pounds	907 g

Appendix 2 Air Fryer Cooking Chart

Beef

Item	Temp (°F)	Time (mins)	Item	Temp (°F)	Time (mins)
Beef Eye Round Roast (4 lbs.)	400 °F	45 to 55	Meatballs (1-inch)	370 °F	7
Burger Patty (4 oz.)	370 °F	16 to 20	Meatballs (3-inch)	380 °F	10
Filet Mignon (8 oz.)	400 °F	18	Ribeye, bone-in (1-inch, 8 oz)	400 °F	10 to 15
Flank Steak (1.5 lbs.)	400 °F	12	Sirloin steaks (1-inch, 12 oz)	400 °F	9 to 14
Flank Steak (2 lbs.)	400 °F	20 to 28			

Chicken

Item	Temp (°F)	Time (mins)	Item	Temp (°F)	Time (mins)
Breasts, bone in (1 ¼ lb.)	370 °F	25	Legs, bone-in (1 ¾ lb.)	380 °F	30
Breasts, boneless (4 oz)	380 °F	12	Thighs, boneless (1 ½ lb.)	380 °F	18 to 20
Drumsticks (2 ½ lb.)	370 °F	20	Wings (2 lb.)	400 °F	12
Game Hen (halved 2 lb.)	390 °F	20	Whole Chicken	360 °F	75
Thighs, bone-in (2 lb.)	380 °F	22	Tenders	360 °F	8 to 10

Pork & Lamb

Item	Temp (°F)	Time (mins)	Item	Temp (°F)	Time (mins)
Bacon (regular)	400 °F	5 to 7	Pork Tenderloin	370 °F	15
Bacon (thick cut)	400 °F	6 to 10	Sausages	380 °F	15
Pork Loin (2 lb.)	360 °F	55	Lamb Loin Chops (1-inch thick)	400 °F	8 to 12
Pork Chops, bone in (1-inch, 6.5 oz)	400 °F	12	Rack of Lamb (1.5 – 2 lb.)	380 °F	22

Fish & Seafood

Item	Temp (°F)	Time (mins)	Item	Temp (°F)	Time (mins)
Calamari (8 oz)	400 °F	4	Tuna Steak	400 °F	7 to 10
Fish Fillet (1-inch, 8 oz)	400 °F	10	Scallops	400 °F	5 to 7
Salmon, fillet (6 oz)	380 °F	12	Shrimp	400 °F	5
Swordfish steak	400 °F	10			

Vegetables

INGREDIENT	AMOUNT	PREPARATION	OIL	TEMP	COOK TIME
Asparagus	2 bunches	Cut in half, trim stems	2 Tbsp	420°F	12-15 mins
Beets	1½ lbs	Peel, cut in ½-inch cubes	1Tbsp	390°F	28-30 mins
Bell peppers (for roasting)	4 peppers	Cut in quarters, remove seeds	1Tbsp	400°F	15-20 mins
Broccoli	1 large head	Cut in 1-2-inch florets	1Tbsp	400°F	15-20 mins
Brussels sprouts	1lb	Cut in half, remove stems	1Tbsp	425°F	15-20 mins
Carrots	1lb	Peel, cut in ¼-inch rounds	1 Tbsp	425°F	10-15 mins
Cauliflower	1 head	Cut in 1-2-inch florets	2 Tbsp	400°F	20-22 mins
Corn on the cob	7 ears	Whole ears, remove husks	1 Tbps	400°F	14-17 mins
Green beans	1 bag (12 oz)	Trim	1 Tbps	420°F	18-20 mins
Kale (for chips)	4 oz	Tear into pieces,remove stems	None	325°F	5-8 mins
Mushrooms	16 oz	Rinse, slice thinly	1 Tbps	390°F	25-30 mins
Potatoes, russet	1½ lbs	Cut in 1-inch wedges	1 Tbps	390°F	25-30 mins
Potatoes, russet	1lb	Hand-cut fries, soak 30 mins in cold water, then pat dry	½ -3 Tbps	400°F	25-28 mins
Potatoes, sweet	1lb	Hand-cut fries, soak 30 mins in cold water, then pat dry	1 Tbps	400°F	25-28 mins
Zucchini	1lb	Cut in eighths lengthwise, then cut in half	1 Tbps	400°F	15-20 mins

Appendix 3 Index

Made in United States
Troutdale, OR
10/10/2023

13579953R00051